THE SUPREME COURT BUILDING, JERUSALEM

THE SUPREME COURT BUILDING, JERUSALEM

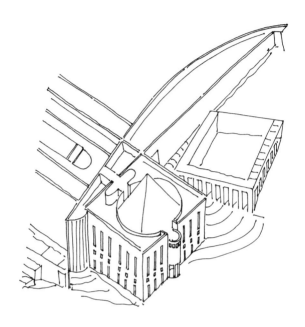

Client: Yad Hanadiv

Architects: Ada Karmi-Melamede, Ram Karmi

Construction coordinator and supervisor: Eliezer Rahat

Initial planning and budget consultant: Dan Wind

Contractor: G.G. Peretz, Engineers

ACKNOWLEDGMENTS

*I*ncluded in this book is only a fraction of the material I gathered in innumerable conversations. Many of those on the long list of professionals involved in the project provided important information and also made a point of touring the site with me. I am deeply indebted to Ada Karmi-Melamede and Ram Karmi; project architects Meir Drezner (project supervisor at Karmi Architects, Ltd., Tel Aviv), Iftach Issacharov and Simone Friedman (senior architects), and design team Alan Aranoff, Motty Shyovitz, Rami Yogev and Zvi Dunsky; Supreme Court President Meir Shamgar, who made available letters and documents relating to the course of construction; Court Registrar Shmuel Tsur, who was always accessible when help was needed; archaeologist Yizhar Hirschfeld; Micha Levin; Vivianne Barsky; Nelly Kopit; construction supervisor Eliezer Rahat; general contractor Gabriel Peretz; Yair Lorberbaum of the Shalom Hartman Institute and Professor Gabi Cohen. For their assistance in producing this book, special thanks are due to Hava Mordohovich for the design, Yempa Boleslavsky for her editorial work, and Richard Bryant for his most distinguished photography. I also wish to express my gratitude to the staff of Yad Hanadiv in Jerusalem: Marcia Lebeau, Moshe Berlin, Ariel Weiss, Joseph Nevo, Kay Burde, Zahava Hanoch, Oshra Meltzer, Michal Magora, Natania Isaak, Lynn Lavie and Yad Hanadiv architectural adviser Arthur Spector with whom I consulted. I am particularly indebted to Arthur Fried.

Written and compiled by Yosef Sharon
Translation: Alexandra Mahler

Graphic Design and Production: Hava Mordohovich
Photography: Richard Bryant

Additional Photography: Neil Fohlberg, Avraham Hai,
Tal Karmi, Joseph Nevo, Peter Szmuk
Aerial Photography: Albatross Aerial Photography Ltd.

Phototypesetting: Yoel Biran, Ltd.
Reprography: Tafsar Ltd., Jerusalem
Printing: Eli Meir Press, Ltd., Petach-Tikva
Binding: Keter Enterprises, Ltd., Jerusalem

בית המשפט העליון
محكمة العدل العليا
THE SUPREME COURT OF ISRAEL

Public Affairs Department   قسم العلاقات العامة   המחלקה לקשרי חוץ

The Supreme Court of Israel

The Supreme Court Building

With the establishment of the State of Israel in 1948, The Supreme Court was housed in an old, rented building in Jerusalem's Russian Compound. In 1984, Dorothy de Rothschild proposed to the government of Israel that Yad Hanadiv (The Rothschild Foundation) donate a permanent structure for The Supreme Court of Israel in Kiryat David ben Gurion, the government center in Jerusalem. The new building would commemorate the work in Israel of Dorothy's husband James and of her father-in-law, Baron Edmund de Rothschild (*Hanadiv Hayadua, t*he "well-known benefactor"). Ram Karmi and his sister Ada Karmi-Melamede, from Tel Aviv, won the architectural competition held in 1986.

A Tour of the Supreme Court

The building incorporates several contrasts: inside and outside, old and new, lines and circles.

- Inside and Outside: Natural light and walled spaces suggest inside and outside areas.
- Old and New: Architectural elements from Israel's history, and in particular from the history of Jerusalem, are found throughout the building.
- Lines and Circles: Concepts of law and justice are expressed visually. Lines represent law and circles represent justice. "You are righteous… and Your laws are straight" (Psalms : 119:137); "He leads me in the circles of justice" (Psalms 23:3).

The Main Entrance

Visitors face a stairway that resembles an old Jerusalem street. The wall of unhewn stone on the right is similar to walls of buildings in ancient Jerusalem. Mirrors in the open space at the base of this wall create the illusion that the building's foundation extends deep into the earth. This effect recalls the foundations of the Old City of Jerusalem and suggests that the roots of law and justice are also deep. The wall on the left is modern, white and unadorned.

The Panoramic Window

The curved window at the top of the stairs floods the area with natural light and provides a view of the city, including the nineteenth century neighborhood of Nachla'ot, easily recognized by its red roofs. Visitors are now standing on the east-west axis of the building. This axis reflects the growth of the city from east to west. Westward growth is seen in the development of the National Precinct, the site of government buildings including the Knesset, The Supreme Court, the Offices of the Prime Minister, The Bank of Israel and The Ministry.

The Pyramid

Walking toward the library, one enters the pyramid area, a large space that serves as a turning point before the entrance to the courtrooms. This serene space acts as the inner "gate house" of The Supreme Court building. Zacharia's Tomb and Yad Avshalom in the Yehoshafat Valley in Jerusalem inspired the pyramid. Natural light enters round windows at the apex of the pyramid, forming circles of sunlight on the inside walls and on the floor.

רחוב שערי משפט, קריית דוד בן-גוריון, ירושלים 91950
شارع شعري مشباط، كريات دفيد بن جوريون، القدس 91950
Shaarey Mishpat St. Kiryat David Ben-Gurion Jerusalem 91950, Israel
Fax: 02-6527118 :פקס פאكس www.court.gov.il Tel: 02-6759612/3 :טלפון هاتف

בית המשפט העליון
محكمة العدل العليا
THE SUPREME COURT OF ISRAEL

The Library

The library surrounds the pyramid. The volumes, which contain centuries of legal thinking from many countries, embody principles of social justice and moral values. The prominence of the library and its proximity to the entrance to the courtrooms affirms the centrality of law in Jewish history.

The Foyer

The foyer of the courtroom area expresses all the architectural contrasts of the building: inside and outside, old and new, lines and circles. The natural stone wall on the left is a continuation of the wall that begins at the entrance to the building. Courts in biblical times were situated at the gates of the city. "You will appoint judges and officers in all your gates . . . and they will judge people with a just judgment. . ."(Deuteronomy 16:18). The three-tiered design of the courtroom entrances represents these gates and is reminiscent of the three-tiered design used for entrances to many public buildings in the ancient Near East. On the right, in striking contrast to the rough stone wall, is a modern white wall with high niches and seating for the public. Natural light enters these niches through pyramid-shaped skylights and creates changing shadows on the white walls during the day.

The Courtrooms

While the courtrooms differ in size and interior design, their basic structure is similar. Natural light enters through skylights located between the outer walls and the columns. The columns themselves suggest a separation between inside and outside. Each courtroom (except Courtroom 1) has a prisoners' dock and a press box. A law clerk and a stenographer sit at a small desk just below the Justices' dais. Lawyers sit at the semi-circular table facing the Justices. Visitors may enter the courtrooms during the proceedings, but must observe rules of conduct. **Please turn off all electrical equipment such as cell phones and pagers and do not take photographs during court proceedings.**

The Knesset Passageway

On the way to the Courtyard of the Arches the visitor passes a window overlooking the passageway to the Knesset. This path, on the north-south axis of the building, represents both the connection and the separation between the legislative and the judicial branches of government.

The Symbols

At the entrance to the administrative wing, visitors pass a wall design consisting of nine symbols representing various areas of the Court. Each symbol is made of a building material used in the area depicted.

The Courtyard of the Arches

The Justices' chambers, located on the top floor of the building above the Courtyard of the Arches, are not open to the public. The Justices are thereby able to work in a quiet environment, separated from the litigants who appear before them. Each chamber consists of an office for law clerks, one for a secretary and a separate office for the Justice.

The courtyard, made of stone, suggests the arid conditions of the desert that borders Jerusalem. A narrow water channel bisects the Courtyard. The arches resemble the gates of Jerusalem during the Roman Period. The stone quarried from the earth and the water reflecting the sky represent the biblical symbols of truth and justice. The Courtyard of the Arches is inspired by a verse from Psalms, "Truth will spring up from the earth and justice will be reflected from the heavens" (Psalms 85:12).

בית המשפט העליון
محكـمة العـدل العـليــا
THE SUPREME COURT OF ISRAEL

NOTICE TO VISITORS

Welcome to The Supreme Court of Israel. We ask that you observe the following rules:

1. Please preserve the decorum of the Court; loud conversation disturbs staff as well as other visitors and detracts from the dignity of the Court.

2. **Please turn off all cellular phones and pagers.**

3. Please respect the building. Take care not to damage the premises in any way.

4. Please supervise your own children. They should remain close to you and not be allowed to wander on their own.

5. Please eat and drink **only** in the cafeteria, which is open to the public.

6. Please do not smoke. Smoking is allowed **only** in designated outside areas.

7. Please do not talk as you enter a courtroom. Take a seat immediately and do not stand in the aisle. **Photographs are not allowed in a courtroom that is in session.**

8. Please follow the instructions of the security personnel.

Visiting hours: Sunday through Thursday   **8:30 a.m. to 2:30 p.m.**
            Hebrew Tours: **11 a.m.**
            English Tours: **12 Noon**

Groups of more than 10 people must make reservations in advance with The Department of Public Affairs: Tel: 02-675-9612/3   Fax: 02-652-7118

רחוב שערי משפט, קריית דוד בן-גוריון, ירושלים 91950
شارع شعري مشباط، كريات دفيد بن جوريون، القدس 91950
Shaarey Mishpat St. Kiryat David Ben-Gurion Jerusalem 91950, Israel
Fax: 02-6527118 :פקס פאكس www.court.gov.il Tel: 02-6759612/3 :טלפון هاتف

MAP OF THE PUBLIC FLOORS

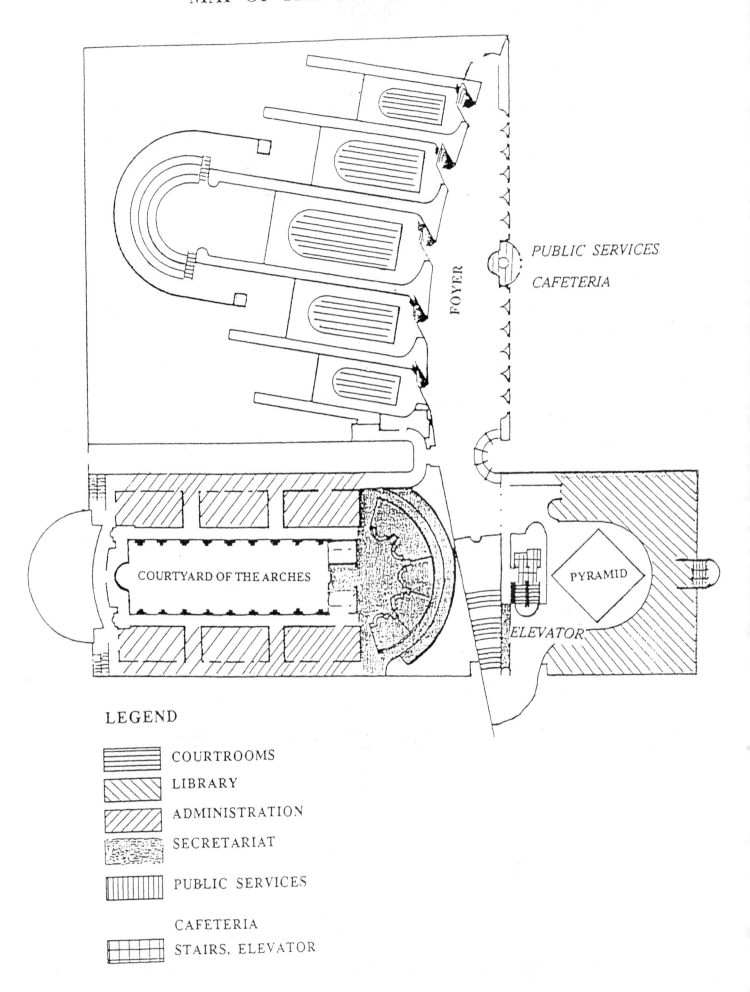

PUBLIC SERVICES

CAFETERIA

FOYER

COURTYARD OF THE ARCHES

PYRAMID

ELEVATOR

LEGEND

COURTROOMS

LIBRARY

ADMINISTRATION

SECRETARIAT

PUBLIC SERVICES

CAFETERIA

STAIRS, ELEVATOR

Children's Tour of the Supreme Court

Welcome to The Supreme Court of Israel.

Ready for a tour with us? Let's go . . .

There are three contrasts that you will see in the building:

1. Inside and Outside

Look around you. Although you are inside, you get the feeling that you are outside because the light from the window at the top of the stairs is so strong.

Throughout the building, you will be in places where you will feel as if you are walking in Jerusalem. What's so special about Jerusalem? There are open places filled with light and narrow places, like alleys, where there is much less light. If it's a busy day in the Court, you will even be surrounded by noise and all kinds of people.

The feeling that we are inside and outside at the same time reminds us that the legal decisions made inside The Supreme Court influence the lives of people outside the Court.

2. Old and New

As you walk up the stairs, look at the walls on your right and on your left. Do you see a difference between the two walls? Can you see that one wall looks old and there is no mortar (cement) between the stones? This wall reminds us of the history of Jerusalem. Around two thousand years ago The Western Wall was built by King Herod. King Herod's workers placed large stones on top of one another without using mortar.

Notice that in the space between the stairs and the wall on your right there are mirrors. **Look down.** What do you see? Yourself? What else? The upper wall is reflected in the mirrors. You have the feeling that the foundations of the building are very deep, just like the foundations of the walls of the Old City of Jerusalem. The architects wanted to tell us that the foundations of law and justice are also very deep.

Go on...

Look at the wall on your left. It is modern and white. As you walk through the building, you will see places that remind us of both ancient and modern times.

Look at the picture of the two walls. One is the Western Wall and one is the main wall of The Supreme Court. Which is which? (1. The right answer is on the last page.)

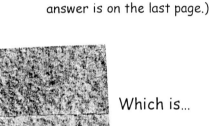

Which is…

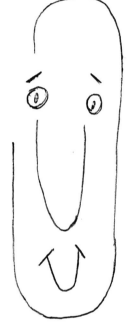

Which?

Panoramic Window:

When you stand here at this window notice that the stone wall on your right extends beyond the window and is both inside and outside at the same time.

Look through the window. Enjoying the view of Jerusalem? The neighborhood with red roofs is called "Nahla'ot" and is one of the oldest neighborhoods outside the Old City walls.

3. Lines and Circles

Turn around and look at the stairway leading to the Justices' chambers. (Judges who serve in The Supreme Court are called Justices.) Notice that the stairway is a straight line.

The straight line represents "**law**." In the Book of Psalms, we read the verse: "*You are righteous... and your laws are straight*", (Psalms: 119:13). (תהילים קי"ט) "צדיק אתה ה' וישר משפטיך". We know that "laws" make sure we stay on a straight path.

Next to the stairs you see a wall in the shape of a half circle. Circles represent "justice". A judge takes the law and *interprets* it so that he or she can apply the law fairly to each case. In the Book of Psalms we read the verse: "*He leads me in circles of justice . . .*" (Psalms: 23:3). (תהילים כ"ג) "ינחני במעגלי צדק למען שמו".

We know that the idea of justice allows the Judge to think about the situation of the person being judged.

From now on, try to find other lines and circles on your own.

The Pyramid and the Library

You have now come to the area that is the formal entrance to the Court. **Look behind you** and you see you have come from "outside" to "inside." **Look up** and you see light coming in from round windows. Where are the straight lines? Where are the circles?

Carry on...

Here are 3 different pyramids. Which is The Supreme Court pyramid? Do you know what the other two are? (2. The right answers are on the last page.)

Go to the windows of the library.

You will see three floors of books. In the library, lawyers use the first floor, Justices use the second floor and retired Justices use the third floor.

Judges in Israel must retire at the age of 70 and may not rule on cases. Retired Justices of The Supreme Court have the honor of keeping an office in the library.

Continue walking...

Court Schedule

As you turn the corner you will see six computer screens on the wall in front of you.

The computers tell people where and when a case is being heard.

The Foyer and Courtrooms

Continue walking. When you turn the corner you will see a big open area with courtrooms on the left side and windows on the right side. **Look at the wall made of Jerusalem stone.** Notice entrances to five different courtrooms.

The entrances remind us of the gates to Jerusalem because in the time of the Bible, judges really did sit at the gates of the city. As we read in Deuteronomy: "*You will appoint judges and officers in all your gates,*" (Deuteronomy 16:18).

"שופטים ושוטרים תיתן לך בכל שעריך... ושפטו את-העם משפט-צדק" (דברים טז')

Cases were decided in the open for everyone to see.

<u>Look at all these gates. Which one is in The Supreme Court?</u>
<u>Would you add it to the 8 gates of Jerusalem? Why?</u>
(3. The right answer is on the last page.)

We hope that one of the courtrooms will be open and
you will be able to see a court in session. In order to
understand what you are about to see, please sit down
on the benches opposite and read about the legal
system.

Enjoying the tour?

There are three levels of courts in Israel. The Magistrates' Court, the District Court and The Supreme Court.

```
                    ┌─────────────────────────────────┐
                    │   The Supreme Court of Israel    │
                    └─────────────────────────────────┘
                      /                              \
┌──────────────────────────┐          ┌──────────────────────────┐
│ The highest Court of Appeals │      │  The High Court of Justice │
└──────────────────────────┘          └──────────────────────────┘
```

Appeals on decisions from the District Courts

Petitions against an injustice by the State

┌──────────────────────────┐
│   The 5 District Courts   │
└──────────────────────────┘

(*Haifa, Nazareth, Tel Aviv, Jerusalem, Be'er Sheva*)

┌──────────────────────────┐
│ The 30 Magistrates' Courts │
└──────────────────────────┘

<u>The Two Roles of The Supreme Court:</u>

1. The Supreme Court of Israel is the highest court of appeals:

What is an appeal?
An appeal is a request to a higher court to check the decision of a lower court and to correct a mistake or an injustice.

<u>Let's take an example from school</u>.

Imagine you are at school and your teacher gives you your grades on an exam. You do not think the grade is fair.

What would you do?

You might ask the teacher to check the exam again or you might go to the assistant principal to complain. You would ask the assistant principal to check your exam again. You hope that you will be given a higher grade. The process that you have just gone through is called an appeal.

HOW TO APPEAL?

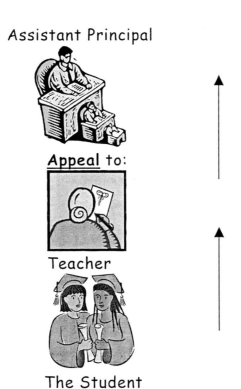

Assistant Principal

Appeal to:

Teacher

The Student

In the legal system the process is similar. A person, who has a case in the Magistrates' Court and loses, can appeal to the District Court. A person, who has a case in the District Court and loses, can appeal to The Supreme Court of Israel.

2. The Supreme Court of Israel is also The High Court of Justice.

A person can petition this Court. *What is a petition? A petition is a written request to the High Court of Justice that asks the Court to help solve an injustice caused by the government.*

Let's take an example:

In 1993 Shahar Butsair's father brought a petition (request) to The High Court of Justice against the Ministry of Education. Shahar was a 13 year-old boy who had to use an electric wheelchair. He complained to the principle of the school that he needed an elevator to get from his classroom on the top floor of the school building to the bathroom on the ground floor.

The principal said he was unable to help him, Shahar and his family complained to many other people involved in the school system and eventually they even sent a letter of complaint to the Minister of Education.

Shahar's family believed that Shahar deserved to have an elevator in the school because he had the right to move easily around the school just like all the other children. The Minister of Education did not agreed to put an elevator in the school and so Shahar and his family petitioned the High Court of Justice against the Ministry of Education.

The High Court of Justice

Ministry of Education

School principal

Shahar Butsair

As a result of the case, an elevator was installed in the school.

A child cannot be humiliated and his independence cannot be taken from him/her. Shahar Butsair's petition helped many other physically challenged children in Israel.

The Courtroom

Please enter the Courtroom quietly.

You cannot take pictures. If you have a cellular phone or a pager, please turn it off.

Here is a picture of the largest courtroom 3-(ג)

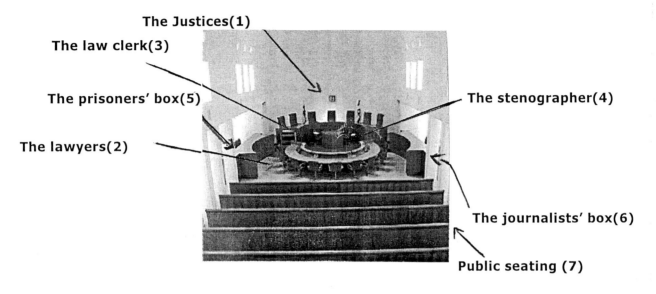

The Justices(1)

The law clerk(3)

The prisoners' box(5)

The lawyers(2)

The stenographer(4)

The journalists' box(6)

Public seating (7)

Justices (1): There are twelve permanent and two temporary Supreme Court Justices and they usually sit in panels of three. They may sit in any odd-numbered panel, 3, 5, 7 etc., depending on the seriousness, difficulty or uniqueness of a case. The decision is made according to the majority.

Lawyers (2): They argue cases.

Law clerks (3): They have completed law school and are training to be lawyers.

Stenographers (4): They record what happens during a court case.

Prisoners' dock (5): Prisoners appeal their convictions or punishments. Prisoners sit in the box with prison guards, but they do not come in handcuffs.

Press box (6): Journalists report to the public on what is going on in the courtrooms.

If you are sitting in the courtroom, you are in the area that was built for the public, for people who bring civil appeals or petitions to The High Court of Justice, and for families of the prisoners (7).

Try to figure out what sort of case you are watching. If you see prisoners in the dock, you can be sure you are watching a criminal appeal.

Please leave the courtroom quietly and turn to the right. Go past Courtroom No. 1 (marked "א" in Hebrew) and go right again. You are looking out a window towards the Knesset. Turn to the left and go around the corner. You will see nine squares.

The Nine Squares

The symbols on these squares represent nine different areas of the Court. Turn left and make a right turn out the door to the Courtyard of the Arches.

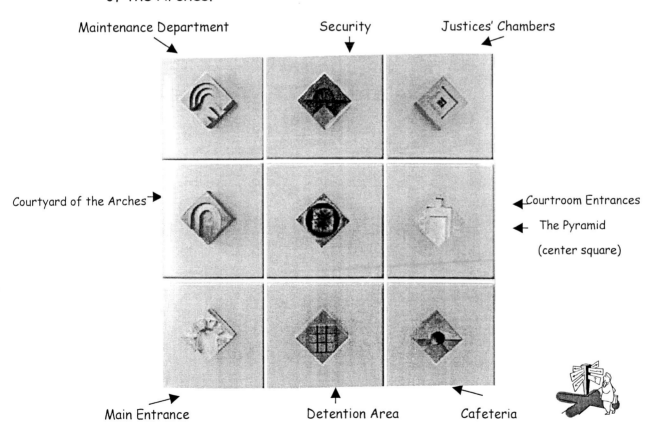

Maintenance Department

Security

Justices' Chambers

Courtyard of the Arches

Courtroom Entrances

The Pyramid (center square)

Main Entrance

Detention Area

Cafeteria

The Courtyard of the Arches

You are now standing in the Courtyard of the Arches. Throughout the building we have seen architectural examples from different periods of Jerusalem's history. The arches remind us of Jerusalem during Roman times. Look at the stone in the center of the arch.

This is called the "keystone," which the Romans invented so that they could build arches without support in the middle.

Look up. Through the windows on the second floor, you can see the area of the Justices' chambers. Justices have their own offices and an area where their staff work. On the level of the Courtyard you can see the legal and administrative offices of the Court.

The architects wanted visitors to this Courtyard to feel like they were in the desert so they used natural light and stone from the Negev. The Courtyard reminds us that "The Law" (The Ten Commandments) was given in the desert.

The channel of water is very narrow, reminding us that there is very little water in the desert. Do you notice something else about the channel of water? (Hint: **Look at the shapes that you see.**)

Notice that the sky is reflected in the water. This reminds us of the verse from The Book of Psalms, "*Truth will spring up from the earth and justice will be reflected from the heavens,*" (Psalms 85:12). "אמת מארץ תצמח וצדק משמים נשקף" (תהילים פ"ה)

It's  for us to leave you...

We hope you have enjoyed looking at and learning about The Supreme Court of Israel. Goodbye.

If you have any questions, talk to one of the staff members or the Department of Public Affairs or call us at (02) 675-9612/3.

Produced by Marcia Greenman Lebeau, Nicole Goldstein Strassman, David Moatti, Bat-El Danous, Daphne Unterschlag and Irena Glatman.

Answer 1: The wall from The Supreme Court is the one on the left.

Answer 2: The pyramid on the left is Absalom's Pillar; the pyramid in the middle is the Pyramid of Giza in Egypt; the pyramid on the right is in The Supreme Court.

Answer 3: The left gate is the Golden Gate, the middle one is the Lions' Gate and the right one is the entrance to the courtrooms at The Supreme Court.

TABLE OF CONTENTS

Lord Rothschild's Forward   7

Yad Hanadiv and the Supreme Court Building   8

The Architectural Competition   23

The Building as a Process   35

The Planning Team   56

The Entrance   75

The Pyramid – A Gatehouse   87

The Library   91

The Grand Foyer   93

The Stone Wall   96

Hierarchy and Light   101

The Courtrooms   102

The Courtyard: Administration Level   115

The Courtyard from the Judges' Level   123

Building and Construction Details   129

The White Stone   176

Afterword   181

Appendix (Architects' Statement of Intent)   187

When my cousin Dorothy de Rothschild first suggested to the Trustees of Yad Hanadiv that she hoped to realize her long-cherished dream, and that of her late husband James, by providing a new building for the Supreme Court, it was immediately apparent that this would be a daunting, but above all a joyful undertaking. The paramount goal of my cousins, and Baron Edmond before them, was to help establish a solid base on which the people of Israel could raise their fledgling state. To this end, our family's foundations have established educational, cultural and religious institutions all over Israel. It was my cousin Jimmy who bequeathed funds to erect the Knesset building. Building the Supreme Court therefore seemed fitting to mark the one hundredth anniversary of Baron Edmond de Rothschild's work in Eretz Yisrael.

In searching for a suitable design, we realized that not only the site but the nature of the city would profoundly affect the selection of architects worthy of the task. Jerusalem is a city of astonishing contrasts, where ancient traditions meet state-of-the-art technology; to give expression to its unique symbolic and spiritual identity proved to be the greatest challenge of the architectural competition won by Ada Karmi-Melamede and Ram Karmi. They have achieved an exceptional blending of tradition and innovation whilst enshrining the relationship between the Law and the Land of Israel. I am confident that future generations will regard this building as a most distinguished architectural work.

As Chairman of the Trustees of Yad Hanadiv, it has been a source of great pride and an enormous honour for me to have inherited from my forebears the tradition of philanthropic work in Israel. I hope that this, our most recent undertaking, does justice to the enormity of their achievements over the past hundred years. One single note of sadness is that Dorothy de Rothschild, whose imagination and wisdom was the force behind this achievement, is not able to see it in its finished glory. I am sure she would have been delighted with the result.

Lord Rothschild

YAD HANADIV AND THE SUPREME COURT BUILDING

With the completion of the Supreme Court in 1992, the various branches of Israel's government are concentrated at a single site in the nation's capital, Jerusalem. The Supreme Court Building stands in close proximity to the Knesset, the Prime Minister's Office, the Bank of Israel and government ministries.

The citizens of Israel take pride in the building, which serves as a visual symbol of the rule of law and expresses the aspirations and goals of the State, as set forth in its Declaration of Independence:

"The State of Israel will be open for Jewish immigration and for the Ingathering of the Exiles; it will foster the development of the country for the benefit of all inhabitants; it will be based on freedom, justice and peace as envisaged by the prophets of Israel; it will ensure complete equality of social and political rights to all its inhabitants irrespective of religion, race or sex; it will guarantee freedom of religion, conscience, language, education and culture;..."

The Knesset and the Supreme Court Building are at the centre of ever widening circles, spreading far beyond the site. Both buildings owe their existence to activities begun over 100 years ago by Baron Edmond de Rothschild, who played a vital role in the Jewish people's revival in their national homeland. What started before the turn of the century as the inspiration of one person, Baron Edmond de Rothschild, who purchased lands and assisted the early pioneers of the First and Second Aliya, became a Rothschild family tradition, with each generation making its own unique contribution.

At the time of his death in 1957, Mr. James de Rothschild, the eldest son of Baron Edmond, was preparing a letter to Prime Minister David Ben-Gurion informing him of the liquidation of PICA (the Palestine Jewish Colonization Association), the transfer of its lands to the State of Israel, and a bequest of funds to build the Knesset. This marked the completion of that chapter in the family's philanthropic activity in Israel begun in 1924 with the establishment of PICA, and the start of a new chapter. In a letter dated June 15, 1957 to Prime Minister Ben-Gurion, Dorothy de Rothschild, James' widow, disclosed her husband's decisions and noted that they would be fulfilled. "For myself," she added, "I shall readily examine what contribution it will be possible to make in the fields of science, art and culture."

Soon after the dissolution of PICA, Yad Hanadiv was established with Dorothy de Rothschild serving as chairman of its small board of trustees. Since the late 1950s, the foundation has endeavoured to meet Israel's evolving educational, cultural and scientific needs. Its work has included the establishment of Educational Television, the Open University, the Centre for Educational Technology, the Jerusalem Music Centre in Mishkenot She'ananim and "Hemda" – Centre for Science Education, Tel Aviv-Yafo.

The "well-known Benefactor," Baron Edmond de Rothschild, with his son James, during the latter's service in the British army

James de Rothschild and his wife Dorothy on a visit to Eretz Israel in the 1930's

The first steps towards providing a Supreme Court building were taken in the early 1980s, in anticipation of centennial celebrations marking the establishment of the first agricultural colonies in Israel supported by Baron Edmond. Dorothy de Rothschild sought to commemorate this jubilee with a symbolic gesture – the endowment of a building of national significance. Her letters suggest that prior to his death, her husband had considered providing a building for the Supreme Court or one for the legislature. His decision, as we know, was to endow the Knesset building. It was Dorothy de Rothschild's belief that a building for the Supreme Court would fully realize her late husband's vision. Her initiative and wisdom turned his vision into a reality.

At the end of the 1960s, the Government of Israel decided to provide a new home for the Supreme Court. Since the establishment of the State, the Court had been 'temporarily' housed in rented quarters in Jerusalem's Russian Compound. The limitations of the building, originally constructed to serve as a pilgrims' hostel, and conditions imposed by the Russian Church, which owned the structure, made it impossible to carry out the improvements required by the Court's growing needs. In 1973 the cornerstone was laid for a new Supreme Court building on Mount Scopus. Construction was, however, never begun as the Government failed to allocate the required funds.

When, in 1981, the trustees of Yad Hanadiv first offered to provide a building, they requested a site near the Knesset, a condition Prime Minister Menachem Begin rejected. Apparently, he considered the earlier government decision designating Mount Scopus as the appropriate site, to be binding. The proposed gift was reluctantly put aside.

Until 1992 the Supreme Court was housed in a building belonging to the Russian Orthodox Mission, one of several structures in the area known as the Russian Compound. The complex, built by the Russians in the middle of the nineteenth century, has remained church property. During World War I, when the British entered Palestine, the building took on a secular-administrative character.

The building, which was rented to the British at the time, and which still houses the Magistrate's Court was the Supreme Court's residence for 44 years. The Supreme Court was located in part of the building and was reached via a corridor, which was also used as a waiting and recess area. The spaces beneath the arches along the second story corridor served as benches. From that vantage point one could observe the internal courtyard. The Russian Mission and several Russian monks were quartered in the east wing.

The unique architectural properties of the building, whose structural elements include stone, iron and glass, are familiar. In the modern Supreme Court Building Karmi-Melamede and Karmi sought to 'convey' the same sensation of thick walls which characterized the old Supreme Court, and other buildings in the Russian Compound.

In 1983, shortly after becoming president of the Supreme Court, Justice Meir Shamgar asked Yad Hanadiv to reconsider its offer. The trustees' preference to locate the Court in proximity to the Knesset conformed to Shamgar's own conception that Kiryat Ben-Gurion, the Government, or National, Precinct of Jerusalem, should house all three branches of government: judicial, executive and legislative. If located on Mount Scopus, Israel's highest judicial authority would, Justice Shamgar believed, be overwhelmed by the sprawling Hebrew University campus and inaccessible due to its rather remote location. Prime Minister Yitzhak Shamir weighed the matter and agreed that the Supreme Court's permanent home should be built in the vicinity of the Knesset.

In response, on December 19, 1984, Dorothy de Rothschild sent a letter to Prime Minister Shimon Peres (who had succeeded Yitzhak Shamir), formally renewing the offer of a new Supreme Court building. With her usual modesty, she defined her role as merely ensuring that the building be completed in accordance with her husband's wishes and in the spirit of his earlier bequest. "We see our response to the need for a new Supreme Court building as a development of the work of both my husband and of his father before him," she wrote. "The aim of both was to provide some of the essentials needed by the people of Israel since the days of the First Aliyah. These ideals still animate our Foundation and will, I trust, continue to inspire future generations to come."

Prime Minister Shimon Peres, greatly moved, responded with a letter of gratitude in which he noted: "By its act, Yad Hanadiv is giving to Israel much more than a building. It is a gift that will serve as a repository of justice, enshrining the cherished values of the rule of law whereby Israel lives." He thanked Mrs. de Rothschild in his own name and on behalf of the people and its government. President Shamgar followed suit, expressing

James de Rothschild

Dorothy de Rothschild

the appreciation of the Supreme Court justices, as well as his own. Dorothy de Rothschild was privileged to visit the building site in 1988, shortly before she died.

Yad Hanadiv's trustees considered that they had a duty to the Israeli public to produce a distinguished public building. The Foundation involved itself in every aspect of the creation of the new building, a process which lasted seven years. To ensure that the Court be satisfied with its new home, the justices were included in the planning process.

Yad Hanadiv undertook responsibility for the entire budget, including infrastructure and furnishings. No sum was mentioned, a departure from usual philanthropic practice. The Foundation supervised the project, but the building represents the fruits of a joint venture in which many different parties were involved, all contributing to its success.

Arthur Fried, Yad Hanadiv's Israel-based trustee, in close consultation with Lord Rothschild, was responsible for the project. He carefully followed the design and construction process and was involved in selecting a professional team to supervise the project: Engineers Dan Wind and Eliezer Rahat, general contractor Gabriel Peretz and many technical consultants. Two of his decisions were particularly crucial. The first was to select a site on the ridge of Givat Ram, and not on its eastern slope as originally proposed by the Government. The second was to invite architects Ada Karmi-Melamede and Ram Karmi to participate as a team in the 1986 architectural competition. Arthur Fried turned to the two, even though the brother-and-sister architects had never submitted a joint proposal to an architectural competition.

Their winning entry is a unique and singular story. They developed their concept in the broadest scope, including interior design, furnishing details and landscaping. The building's exterior combines features of traditional local architecture with contemporary concepts. The massive stone walls and detailed work relieve the observer, at least momentarily, of the vagueness of the Israeli identity, as reflected in the country's modern architecture. The building is firmly rooted, both historically and stylistically, in Jerusalem, and not merely in the Government Precinct.

Dorothy de Rothschild on a visit to the Supreme Court site in 1988, with her close friend Maria Brassey and with Arthur Fried, Yad Hanadiv trustee and project director on behalf of the client

On the building site, winter 1988.
Clockwise: Supreme Court President
Meir Shamgar, Arthur Fried, Ram Karmi,
Moshe Berlin, Arthur Spector and Ada
Karmi-Melamede

Every leading architect who built in Jerusalem (Mendelsohn, Harrison, Holiday) fell under the City's spell. In their statement of intent, Karmi-Melamede and Karmi cited the need to make the building a part of the City's cultural and historical context. Their intention was that design transcend vagaries of style and history. Karmi-Melamede and Karmi's plan, based on a horizontal massing, best adapted itself to the ridge. It also fulfilled the important stipulation in the competition brief that equal weight be accorded to the Knesset building, situated to the south of the Supreme Court.

The building's elevations are stark and simple. The north facade is perceived as a city wall and yet the formal expression of the building does not lend itself to unequivocal classification. The structure consists of four distinct parts (library, courtrooms, judges' chambers and parking area), each symmetrical in itself and linked by a major flowing space. The building evokes ancient structures like Absalom's Tomb in the Kidron Valley, synagogues and Byzantine churches, while paying homage to the Rockefeller Museum and to the arched vaults of Government House (the seat of the High Commissioner of Palestine during the British Mandate).

For appellants and petitioners, the new building, like its predecessor in the Russian Compound, is a place entered by necessity, although it merits a visit solely for the architectural experience. The architects' original plan for a building divided into four parts and including a spacious public level pre-empted a palatial structure. The law as a normative principle in both individual and public life was the architects' main consideration; the building accords it great respect.

The long entrance leading to the courtrooms, and the stepped transition from the Jerusalem exterior to the building's interior, start as an alley and develop into a large public domain. This sequence suggests the complex affiliations to archaic motifs, to Jerusalem elements and to the Israeli landscape. The architects sought to internalize and express the needs of the building's permanent resident, the Supreme Court and, perhaps even more, the expectations of the Israeli public.

15.7.1957.

My dear Prime Minister,

I have often read and re-read the noble and generous words of your cable of condolence. They give me so much comfort in my sorrow.

Now I must turn from my grief and apply myself to the affairs of the P.I.C.A. My husband had, over the last few years, given much thought to the work of P.I.C.A. and its future. He had carefully considered every aspect of the problem and, shortly before his death, prepared a letter to you, in which he set out his conclusions. The letter read as follows:

"My dear Prime Minister,

My father began his colonization work in Israel 75 years ago. The work which was then begun has been continued to this day. When in 1924 my father set up the Palestine Jewish Colonization Association — P.I.C.A. — he assigned to it the task of colonizing all his landholdings. It fell to me to preside over P.I.C.A. ever since its inception.

In the years that followed, the marshes were drained; the rocky hills and barren wastes were turned into fertile soil. All these lands were then colonized by P.I.C.A. Today there is no cultivable land left to P.I.C.A. for further colonization. The task set to P.I.C.A. has been fulfilled.

As I cast my eyes back over our work, I think that I may fairly say that we have adhered to two principles which well bear restating:

the first, that we did our work without regard to political considerations,

and the second, that we endeavoured to give to Israel and her people all that we could, without seeking anything in return — neither profits, nor gratitude, nor anything else.

The colonizing task of P.I.C.A. having been fulfilled, the question that lay before me was to decide on the future of P.I.C.A. The State of Israel has since been created and the National Institutions have emerged to take over the major colonization effort in Israel.

Weighing all the elements, I have reached the conclusion that, with the completion of its task, the right course would be to terminate the activities of P.I.C.A., instead of duplicating the work which is done now, on a far larger scale, by the National Institutions.

P.I.C.A. is a private association, but all its efforts have been directed to the benefit of the public. For this reason I thought it right to inform you of my decision first. For the same reason, I also propose to transfer now all the remaining P.I.C.A. lands (leased and not leased) to National Institutions.

I look upon the termination of P.I.C.A.'s work as a mark of fulfilment, not as a withdrawal. I would like to underline this by a special act of identification with the aspirations of Israel and her people. We intend to provide the sum of IL. 6 million for the construction of the new Knesseth building in Jerusalem which, I understand, it is proposed to set up. Let the new Knesseth building become a symbol, in the eyes of all men, of the permanence of the State of Israel.

Letter dated July 15, 1957 from Dorothy de Rothschild to Prime Minister David Ben-Gurion, citing a letter from her late husband, James de Rothschild, in which he offered to provide funds to construct a Knesset Building

With this done, P.I.C.A. will withdraw from the scene of Israel in the knowledge that the work which was begun 75 years ago is being carried on by the State and the people, supported by world Jewry.

With this letter I meant to inform you of my decision. I do not intend, with this letter, to take leave of you or of Israel. My interest in the development of Israel is abiding. Even if P.I.C.A. must cease to operate, I shall remain as close to you all as I have always been. Your cares will be my cares and your happiness will be my happiness.

Indeed, I shall want to examine whether I shall be able to make some modest contribution, in the future, towards the advancement of science, art and culture in Israel — all matters which, I know, are near to your heart. However, these are but thoughts for the future. I am not yet fully decided on them but may revert to them as soon as these thoughts become crystallized in my own mind.

The foundations of the State have been well and truly laid. I am confident that, by the grace of the Almighty, the new chapter in the history of our people which began with the creation of the State, will be glorious and enduring.

Yours sincerely."

Alas, with this letter, my husband took leave of you and of Israel and it has now fallen to me and the Council to execute what he had resolved.

I need hardly say that the contribution of IL. 6 million for the new Knesseth building will be provided. Let me add that this was a project to which my husband attached especial significance.

For myself I shall readily examine what contribution it will be possible to make in the fields of science, art and culture which are mentioned in the letter. I cannot say at the moment what will prove feasible but I can assure you that everything that can be done will be done.

Before concluding let me add that my husband always thought and spoke of you with the greatest affection and respect. In all his work for Israel, he was greatly inspired by your example and by the exertions of the whole people of Israel.

Believe me, my dear Prime Minister,

Yours sincerely,

(Sgd.) Dorothy de Rothschild.

December 19ᵗ 1984

Dear Prime Minister

May I write to you on a subject which is very near my heart as I feel sure it is near yours — it concerns the building of a new Supreme Court of Justice on a site worthy of its national importance, to replace the present Court's inadequate premises in a leased building in the Russian Compound.

Just before my husband died in 1957, it was his wish to offer the State of Israel a building either for the use of its Parliament or its Supreme Court. He realised how greatly either would symbolise the basic principles of the State of Israel.

In the event the Knesset became his first choice and, as a result, I hope you agree, the legislature of Israel has a home worthy of its task.

I have been asked by the Council of our Foundation Yad Hanadiv, to tell you that we would like to offer the State of Israel a new Supreme Court building and thus fully realise my husband's vision of some 27 years ago.

I have just heard that a site near the Knesset could now be made available for this purpose. We are indeed deeply appreciative of this decision as we attach great importance to the proximity of the two buildings — together they would embrace Israel's fundamental attachment both to Justice & Democracy.

Should your Government look favourably on our proposal, Yad Hanadiv would undertake to fund the entire cost of the new Court's planning, development, construction & equipment,

16

Working in co-operation with the President of the Supreme Court — your belief that this proposal would be for the benefit of Israel would be the signal for the work to be started as soon as possible —

We see our response to the need for a new Supreme Court as a development of the work of both my husband and of his father before him — The aim of both was to provide some of the essentials needed by the people of Israel since the days of the First Aliyah — These ideals still animate our Foundation and will, I trust, continue to inspire future generations to come —

The words of the Prophet Isaiah read :—

"And I will restore your judges
as at first, and your counsellors
as at the beginning — Afterwards
Jerusalem shall be called
The City of righteousness
and a faithful city"

Mercifully these words have stood the test of time. If through the creation of the new Supreme Court, these ideals might, in some measure, be helped by Yad Hanadiv, we would indeed feel we were continuing the traditions set by our founders —

Yours most Sincerely
Dorothy de Rothschild .

Letter dated December 19, 1984 from Dorothy de Rothschild, in which she officially informed Prime Minister Shimon Peres of Yad Hanadiv's decision to provide funds for a Supreme Court Building

Overleaf: *Jerusalem by Moonlight – A View to the South (photograph taken in 1992, towards the end of construction)*

בית המשפט העליון
ירושלים
THE SUPREME COURT OF ISRAEL
JERUSALEM

PRESIDENT'S CHAMBERS

לשכת הנשיא

Jerusalem, December 28th 1984

Dear Lady de Rothschild,

With deep appreciation and gratefulness I am writing to you on behalf of the Israeli judiciary in order to convey to you and to the Council of the Foundation Yad Hanadiv our most profound feelings of gratitude and esteem for the decision on the construction of a building for the Supreme Court of Israel.

This decision as expressed in your kind and moving words in the letter to the Prime Minister is a further manifestation of the unique place of the Foundation and its founders in the history of the renaissance of the Jewish people in its ancient homeland. It signifies your attachment to the spiritual values which have to guide our people and your unwavering efforts to create concrete frameworks which will serve the new Israeli society, shape its trends and further the achievement of its ideals.

Please accept our best wishes and thanks,

Yours most sincerely

M. Shamgar

Letters of gratitude to Dorothy de Rothschild from Prime Minister Shimon Peres and Supreme Court President (Chief Justice) Meir Shamgar, after they were informed of Yad Hanadiv's decision to construct a building for Israel's Supreme Court

20

My dear Lady Dorothy de Rothschild—

It was with profound emotion and a deep sense of gratitude that I read your letter of Dec. 13, 1984, informing me that the Yad Hanadiv foundation has decided to offer the State of Israel a new edifice to house the Supreme court of our country. Your magnanimous gesture is indeed a worthy and lasting monument of historic dimension to the vision of your late beloved husband and to the noble purpose of Yad Hanadiv.

Given the special content of your letter and its unique significance for all of Israel, I thought it proper to accept your communication from the hands of your representatives in the presence of my ministerial colleagues and the President of the Supreme Court. It was a brief and moving ceremony held in my office on Friday, Dec 28. The fact that your letter of offer was written in your own hand made the occasion even more meaningful.

By its act, Yad Hanadiv is giving to Israel much more than a building. It is a gift that will serve as a repository of justice, enshrining the cherished values of the rule of law whereby Israel lives. In Jerusalem, generations of the future will see our Knesset and our Supreme Court, in magnificent appropriate setting side by side, and they will recall that the seat of our democracy and the bastion of our justice were housed in lasting permanence thanks to the vision, generosity and inspiration of your dear late husband, with his nobility of spirit and his humanity, his illustrious father, and of course yourself.

Throughout the history of Israel, the Rothschild family has played the role of a ministering angel. It would be impossible to describe the economic social and educational development of the State of Israel without the intensive involvement of the Rothschild family. Even more, it would be impossible to relate our political history without our "Magna Carta" — the Balfour Declaration delivered to a member of your family.

Your noble act, dear madame, represents yet another stratum in the Zionist edifice. In this, you are providing a magnificent repository for the fulfillment of the hope expressed by the prophet Isaiah:

"And I will restore thy judges as at first, and thy counsellors at the beginning; afterward thou shalt be called, The city of righteousness, the faithful city. Zion shall be redeemed with judgment, and her converts with righteousness."

Isaiah 1:26-27

I have asked our Ambassador, Mr Yehuda Avner, to hand this reply to you personally.

On behalf of the people and Government of Israel, I thank you most sincerely —

Yours

Shimon Peres

2.1.1985

Supreme Court corner-stone laying ceremony (1987). From left to right: *Lord Rothschild, Supreme Court President Meir Shamgar, Foreign Minister Shimon Peres, President Chaim Herzog, Knesset Chairman Shlomo Hillel, Minister of Justice Avraham Sharir and Jerusalem Mayor Teddy Kollek;* Below: *Supreme Court President Meir Shamgar and Dorothy de Rothschild at a 1988 meeting with the architects and the planning team*

THE ARCHITECTURAL COMPETITION

*O*nce the decision was made to provide a building, Yad Hanadiv arranged an international architectural competition in order to elicit proposals from some of the world's finest architects. The specific nature of the competition, i.e. the selection of an architect and not just a plan, was determined after meetings with the organizers of several architectural competitions held in the 1980s. These included Harold Williams, President of the John Paul Getty Foundation (which established the Paul Getty Museum in Malibu), and Dr. Jean Boggs, the organizer of the competition for the Canadian National Gallery in Ottawa. The advice underscored that the success of a project of this scope requires that the client be keenly aware of his needs and expectations. Only then may architects be invited to participate in a competition with confidence that the selection process will yield a satisfactory result.

According to the advice received, the architect's temperament and character determine the outcome no less than does the competition entry. Great weight was therefore placed on interviews with the architects. For the first time in Israel, priority was given to choosing an architect not only on the merits of the plans submitted, but also in anticipation of an on-going dialogue to continue throughout the design process.

Yad Hanadiv considered holding an open competition among architects from Israel and abroad or, alternatively, limiting it to a small number of well-known architects. As the project was of national significance, it was decided to hold a two-stage competition combining both options: a first-stage competition open to all Israeli architects, followed by a second stage to include six invited architects. William Lacey, former President of Cooper Union, presided as chairman of the jury, notwithstanding the Israel Architects' Association's contention that this contravened their rule stipulating that the chairman be selected by their "Competition Committee." The competition programme and procedures were guided by talented Jerusalem architect Arthur Spector, with uncompromising attention to every detail.

Five jurors, all renowned architects and teachers, participated in the first stage of the competition: William Lacey (chairman); Charles Moore, former Dean of the Faculty of Architecture, University of California, Los Angeles; Cesar Pelli, former Dean of the Faculty of Architecture at Yale University; Jerusalem architect David Reznik; and Daniel Havkin, former Dean of the Faculty of Architecture, the Technion – Israel Institute of Technology. In the second stage, which culminated in personal interviews, additional jurors participated: Supreme Court President Meir Shamgar; Sir Isaiah Berlin; Colin Amery, architectural critic of the London-based "The Financial Times," and Lord Rothschild.

The professional challenge and the demands posed by such a unique project attracted 174 Israeli architects to the first stage, despite the dissatisfaction evinced by several members of the Israel Architects' Association at the decision to include invited

Yad Hanadiv offices, Jerusalem Top: *Dorothy de Rothschild greeting Supreme Court Judge Gabriel Bach* Below: *Arthur Spector, architectural consultant to Yad Hanadiv, shaking hands with Dorothy de Rothschild. Between them is Ada Karmi-Melamede.*

architects in the second round. Four architectural firms advanced to the second stage: Hillel Schocken and Uri Shaviv; Amir and Opher Kolker and Randy Epstein; Roni Seibert and Marcel Klugman; and David Shalev. The four first-stage winners were joined in the second round by six invited architectural firms from Israel and abroad. The invitees from Israel were: Ada Karmi-Melamede and Ram Karmi; Yaacov Rechter; and Moshe Safdie. The three foreign architectural offices were: Richard Meier (U.S.A.); James Freed, I.M. Pei and Partners (U.S.A.); and Ricardo Legorreta (Mexico).

In the second stage, held in the early summer of 1986, four firms were selected to be interviewed by the jury: Kolker-Kolker-Epstein (Israel); James Freed, I.M. Pei and Partners (U.S.A.); David Shalev (an Israeli architect with the firm of Evans-Shalev, England); and Ada Karmi-Melamede and Ram Karmi (Israel). The winners were Ada Karmi-Melamede and Ram Karmi.

In their comments on the winning design, the jury emphasized the need for a balance between "adequate dimensions" and an honorific building, between "practical considerations required of the building" and "an understanding of the need for symbolism." They also mentioned "respect for the traditions of Israel," perhaps seeking to denote the relative modesty of the conception favoured, in that the building's eminence is introverted. The jury endorsed Karmi-Melamede and Karmi's "Jerusalem archetypes" and its proposed massive, horizontal facades resembling city walls and recalling buildings from the Mandatory period.

Sitting as the High Court of Justice, the Supreme Court hears challenges to legislative, executive and administrative acts which "by their nature carry implications for the rule of law in Israel in its widest sense because of their significant connection to fundamental questions."[1] The panel did not want a pretentious structure, one liable to create the impression that those sitting in judgment place themselves above the nation's representatives in the Legislature. At the interview stage, architects Karmi-Melamede and Karmi stressed that "the building should not assume power but deserve it." Their proposal was judged to provide the best solution to the "most appropriate image," an image which in the jury's words, respects "the special nature of justice and the traditions of Israel."

The Jewish people does not have an accepted paradigm of a courthouse, a legacy from the past for the modern state. The competition brief noted the need for symbolism in order to generate the greatest number of architectural concepts. Without setting priorities or giving explicit directives, the brief underlined the need for authority and openness, stability and ritual. To provide the jury with an understanding of the architectural concept and its symbolic import, participants were requested to include comprehensive explanations. They were asked to account for their choices of material and form, and to elucidate the symbolism embodied in their plans. All the architects attempted (both in their explanations and at the interviews) to balance the requirements set forth in the brief with the eternally unknown: a perception of the image most appropriate for a supreme court.

The architects had at their disposal Israel's archaeology and the complex character, both new and old, of Jerusalem. This is a mixed blessing; so tight and complex is the link

Ram Karmi explaining the building plan

between the City's different architectural styles and the various national and religious traditions that it would be virtually impossible to isolate a decisively 'Jewish' or 'national' element. In tackling such a unique project, it would be inconceivable to fall back only on what is intrinsic to Jerusalem or familiar in its civic buildings.

Many of the competing architects went back to the 'sources,' especially to the Bible – as asserted in their statements of intent. Their pursuit of meanings and associations (even if these cannot be unequivocally 'rendered' into the language of architecture) reflected the desire to cast aside the fashionable and grasp at any clue, in the hope of finding a Biblical source that would lead to a reasoned choice. This was an unarticulated quest for a modern 'correct model,' not only a representative and 'handsome' courthouse, but one befitting the status of Israel's Supreme Court.

All the proposals showed symbolic affinity to the past. Some architects accentuated the contours of the building and its likeness to an enclave; others emphasized the structure's openness to the heavens, the association with a line and a circle (in the spirit of the Biblical metaphor linking law to a line (Isaiah 28:17) and justice to a circle (Proverbs 2:9)), or to the element of water: "But let judgment run down as waters, and righteousness as a mighty stream" (Amos 5:24). There were those who conferred symbolic significance on the library or the courtrooms. Others suggested designs for the entrance and the gateway which entailed symbolic aspects.

Apart from the Biblical images of law and justice, the concern for symbolism raised an issue never encountered in Scripture. Is it possible to invoke the concept of judicial authority architecturally through an archaic motif, such as the gate? "Judgment in the gate" (Deut. 16:18) actually took place under the skies, in an open, public area. Scripture says nothing about architectural components. The gate was not the judges' place of assembly; judgments were held there because it was a passageway bustling with movement, not because it was 'symbolic.'

The jury meticulously reviewed each statement of intent,[2] without giving preference to proposals originating in Scripture. None of the participants had submitted an 'ideal model,' explicitly related to the Law. Ancient texts and cultural conventions are at one and the same time open to us, yet remote. However, it is the very essence of Judaism to question – in principle, to doubt how a court should be represented. Each of the jurors was forced to fall back on his own intuition. The panel weighed the advantages of each proposal and its possible development. The strength of Karmi-Melamede and Karmi's plan seemed to derive from its relative simplicity and the stability it projected.

Architecture's mystique is the product of the relationship between form and site, time and culture. Combinations are revealed when a building assumes its massing. Not always is the scale definable or self-evident. Although the Supreme Court's status and function are of paramount importance, what scale could properly represent them? It is not by chance that according to tradition an angel holds the measuring rod: "And behold, there was a man... with a line of flax in his hand and a measuring rod; and he stood in the gate" (Ezekiel 40:3).

The competition judges are not angels and they do not wield a holy measuring rod. Certainly, the jury could not presume to know how the project would turn out. The legitimation it accorded to the Karmi-Melamede and Karmi conception was rooted in the feeling that the 'key' to a building befitting the Supreme Court could be found in the urban scale that has always characterized Jerusalem. The panel considered that the design aptly emphasized this aspect of the building: "Its handsome exterior is derived from, and is in harmony with, the character and spirit of Jerusalem."

In press interviews during and after the competition, Karmi-Melamede and Karmi tried to articulate what distinguishes Jerusalem from other cities:

"Throughout the world, monumentality is congruous with power. But not in Jerusalem. Here there is a sense of the 'unknown' rather than of power. You look at buildings, part of which are hidden from view by the city wall. You see their skyline, but not where they touch ground. You always retain the sensation of hidden layers and indefinite heights. This imparts a certain mystique to the buildings. Anywhere else in the world it would be called monumentality."

Karmi-Melamede and Karmi's search for Jerusalem archetypes and their desire to translate them into a built form, led to interesting results on the symbolic level. Their original scheme (see page 32) emphasized the symbolism of the inner gatehouse, enveloped by the library. In refining their concept, they proposed a massive continuous stone wall that bisects the building (see page 54). The wall gave birth to the entrances to the courtrooms; the gate motif, judgment at the gate, was adopted in the design of the five courtrooms and reiterated in the building's interior, rather than in its facades (see page 55). If the intrinsic symbolism of a courthouse has been realized, the prerequisite was the internalization of the City's urban scale (as perceived by the architects).

1. Aloni V. Minister of Justice PD 41(2) p. 1, 29.
2. Additional documentation may be found in the catalogue "The Supreme Court Building, Jerusalem: an architectural competition," The Tel Aviv Museum, 1987.

James Freed

"The 'centre' of the Supreme Court is placed at the crossing of visual (axial) lines from the Israel Museum, the Knesset and the Hilton Hotel. Its orientation is a modest one given its dominant location, and is not captured by a unique relationship to any one of the buildings on the site; rather it acts with them all.

"Conceptually, some finite number of solution types presented themselves. The building could be like a Palazzo, it could be a sculptural marker, it could be Basilican or it could be a courtyard building. As we do not have to cope with an urban situation and since we do not have strong local contextual clues, the courtyard scheme seems desirable. The Supreme Court can make its own environment and its internal court can provide for scale and shelter in this exposed condition.

"The Supreme Court building does not attempt to link itself exclusively with any other building – rather it sets itself free as an institution neither higher nor lower in status than the Knesset building.

"The perception of the processional is crucial, leading as it does from exterior to court, to rotunda/exhibit space, to galleria and, finally, to courtroom. The spaces of the promenade are modified by lighting strategies that flood the interior by freeing internal shells from exterior surroundings."

The Jury's Comments

"This entry was exquisitely delineated and studied with great care and thoroughness – sophisticated in concept, form, materials and lighting. A high level of professionalism was evident in the execution of the project's design philosophy which sought a building with 'symbolic resonance as well as practical use' – a building which, in the architect's words, 'would be timeless with timely furnishings and outlook.'

"The design was commended for its highly developed and orderly plan, for its poetic and skillful use of light, and for the refinement of detail.

"To some members of the jury the monumental nature of the building conveyed an attitude too severe and one inconsistent with the nature of the court. The building seemed to be imposed on the site rather than part of it."

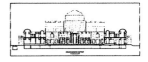

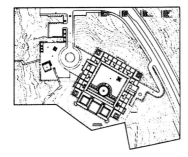

David Shalev

"We have selected an architectural idea which represents: individual equality before the law; perfect balance of deliberation; final authority of judgement.

"The design concept evolved in response to the dual architectural problem presented by the brief: first, to achieve a modern, forward-looking and efficient court building using appropriate traditional architectural elements; second, to establish a coherent plan for Kiryat David Ben-Gurion.

"In our proposal, we attempt to demonstrate our wish to create a building which has a dignified presence, assuming an appropriate scale both internally and externally, and one which is at the same time modest in appearance, welcoming and using simple forms and calm surfaces. A building which functions well and responds to the landscape.

"The spatial organization is appropriate to the solemnity of the occasion. It is formal and ceremonial, whilst establishing a sequence of useful and serene places for all users.

"The proposed building is in scale with the landscape and with the existing buildings in the cluster, stately but unimposing.

"An architectural dialogue with the Knesset is established by similarity of scale. The Supreme Court building is compatible with the Knesset but distinct in character."

The Jury's Comments

"This scheme, selected during the first stage of the competition, showed admirable refinement of an already carefully conceived design. Classic in form and arrangement, clear in its intentions, the proposal has many commendable features. The building has an extremely clear circulation pattern, the proper scale and feeling of an important public building and obviously had been studied in great detail with sensitivity and skill.

"The lack of contact with the natural surroundings and the predictability of the interior spaces was criticized. There was a general feeling that the scheme did not lend itself – as well as some other schemes did – to the degree of further development and change that would be required. The somewhat dated aspect of the design was commented on and the fact that it seemed to place greater emphasis on the pragmatic over the aesthetic. Some members questioned the location of the main courtroom at the uppermost level."

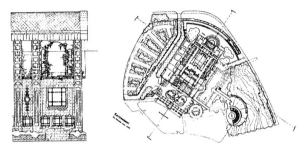

Amir Kolker, Opher Kolker, Randy Epstein

"The promenade follows the line of the ridge and is aligned with the Knesset. It begins with a colonnade between the National Auditorium and the Zionist Archives past the Court Building, the Reception Pavilion and on to the Knesset providing along its route entries to other areas of the National Campus. The promenade gives the campus an architectural identity and a relationship to the urban fabric of the capital.

"The Supreme Court itself is situated on the urban side of the promenade, making it and the Knesset alone the representative elements of the campus toward the city space. The entry pavilion of the Supreme Court building is part of the promenade in its architectural language and orientation. The Court building, however, is rotated to a north-south orientation corresponding to the other buildings on the National Campus and creating a space between the promenade and the Court's outer wall, the "lower plaza."

"The traditional architecture of Jerusalem has also been marked by the contrast between light structural elements – iron and glass – and the heavy stonework. This contrast is manifest in large, filigreed screens and windows, in wrought iron balustrades and iron cantilevered balconies, and in large glass enclosed porches. Above all, building materials in Jerusalem have been tactile and intimate.

"The use of different stone traditions gives distinct character to the various elements of the Supreme Court Building.

"The Supreme Court of Justice is more than just an additional building on the National Campus. Through its inclusion in the promenade, the building is related to the rest of the campus and creates a built edge between campus and city space."

The Jury's Comments

"The work presented by this office is representative of the individuals – intelligent, imaginative, filled with youthful exuberance, but mature in concept and execution.

"The jury found much to recommend this scheme, from its careful analysis of the site and the proposed axial sequences intended to organize it better, to the meticulous and precise arrangements of plan and elevations."

"In the end it was this relentless geometry and undeviating repetition of form and pattern, however, that caused the jury to remove it from consideration.

"Many on the jury, while admiring the skill with which this entry was executed, found that the basic premises did not result in a plan distinctive enough for this special building".

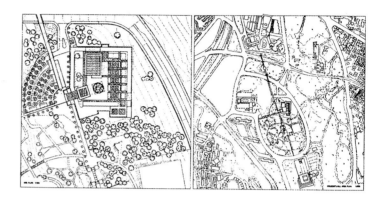

Ada Karmi-Melamede, Ram Karmi

"This building cannot be viewed merely as a single freestanding object in the landscape, but should relate both to its immediate environment and to the larger urban context. Our intention is to create a harmonious relationship among the executive, legislative and judicial institutions and also to create a public place which is part of a larger sequence.

"Public movement towards the building and within, is a combination of circular and linear patterns. The intent is to give a clear geometric expression to the values of justice and law. Justice is described in the Bible as a circle while law is described as a line.

"A grand circular movement which generates from the entry is reinforced by the configuration of the curved library above. This movement is dramatically transformed by the disposition of the courtrooms into a singular linear axis.

"Functionally the building is divided into two systems: horizontal and vertical. The former provides the line between the different domains within the building and defines the boundary between inside and out. The latter creates the hierarchy of public and private and sets up the visual tension between them.

"One ascends towards a 'window', which acts as a turning point from which one confronts the actual entrance hall. This space is reminiscent of Absalom's Tomb as a testimony to the intransigence of law through time. The pure geometrical form of this room tapers towards the apex, allowing light to penetrate its volume. It is a static and serene space which detaches the sacred from the profane. This is the true 'gate-house' of the Supreme Court Building.

"The courtyard is made exclusively of stone, broken only by a narrow channel of water on the central axis."

The Jury's Comments

In the interview session Ada Karmi-Melamede said, "I think we did a good job." The jury agreed.

"This was deemed the best solution to the site – the most agreeable and most sensitive. Its handsome exterior is derived from, and in harmony with, the character and spirit of Jerusalem.

"It is a respectful building – respecting the special nature and problem of the site and justice and the traditions of Israel. It demonstrates an understanding of the need for symbolism but does not ignore the practical considerations required by its various publics.

"Although the jury expressed unanimous admiration for the design, this was accompanied by critical remarks concerning the view from the judges' offices, the somewhat complicated circulation pattern and the appearance of the building as overly suppressed in the landscape. It is a scheme, however, whose potential for change and further development with the client, seemed to hold out the most promise."

31

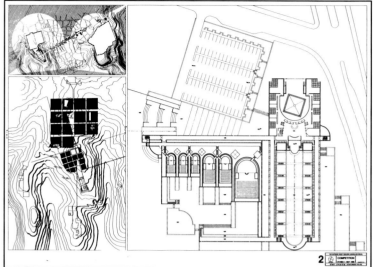

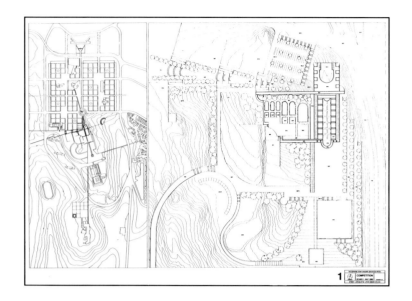

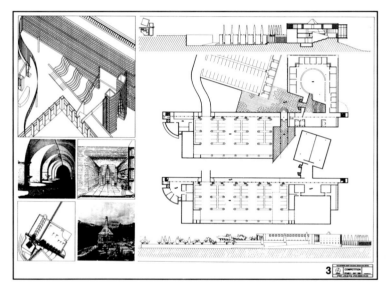

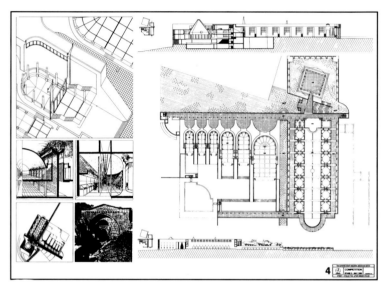

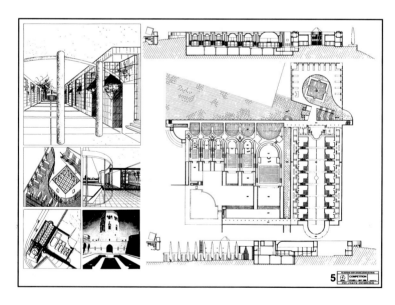

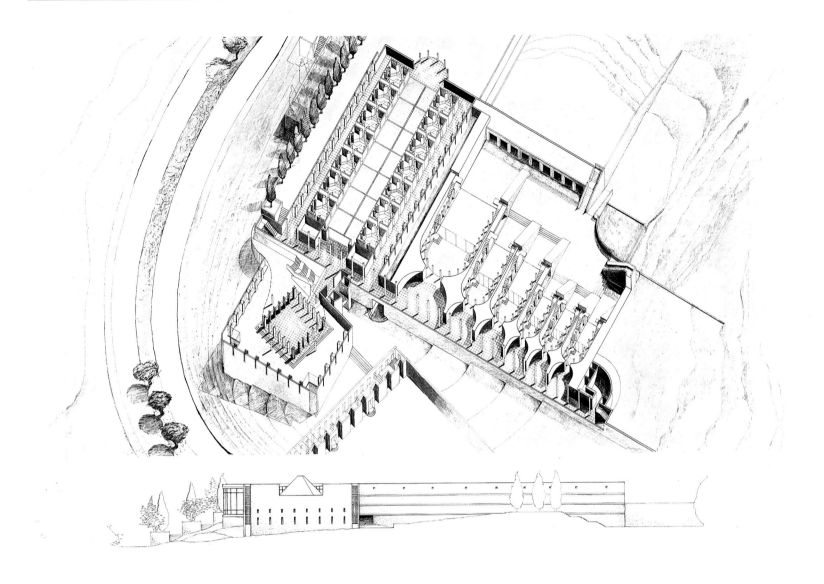

Axonometric view of public circulation (809) Below: *north elevation*

Above right: *The Tomb of Mary, a Byzantine church at the foot of the Kidron Valley, built over burial caves* Above left: *Absalom's Tomb, one of a series of ancient tombs in the Kidron Valley dating to the Second Temple period. The monolith, probably erected at the beginning of the First Century C.E., is divided into two parts: the crypt and the conical structure* Below right: *A passage in the Armenian monastery, Armenian Quarter, the Old City of Jerusalem* Below left: *the Rockefeller Museum – the Eretz Israel Archaeological Museum designed by S.B. Harrison during the Mandatory Period and inaugurated January, 1938*

"THE BUILDING AS A PROCESS"

(From an interview with the architects)

"Jerusalem is not the outgrowth of a sequential or singular design concept. The city was built up around various centres of public activity, dating from different historical periods, and it is these nuclei which create its image. The map of the city, like that of the Supreme Court Building, mirrors a distinct hierarchy of those cores implanted in our individual and collective memories. In the harmonious orchestration of these centres, Jerusalem asserts our identity, as it narrates our origins and continuity.

"We tried to provide a conceptual image of the urban memory and of our deep consciousness of the city in a building whose architecture would reflect the personal map imprinted in each individual. The building was intended to project a feeling of personal possession, just as the city does, and perhaps even of communal possession – in a structure that could suggest cultural orientation and be a source of pride.

"In developing and refining our sixteen schemes*, we adhered to the explicit guidelines of the competition. The motifs that we drew on are derived from a composite urban perception relating to the Supreme Court's specific functions and location in Jerusalem in the heart of the National Precinct. The courthouse was set at the intersection of the coordinates that bisect the building; the east-west axis stretches eastward towards the Old City of Jerusalem and, on the west, reaches back to the Mediterranean Sea. We sought to anchor within its matrix the external urban elements that cross the structure, so that its major public spaces would transcend the building's physical limits.

"Since time immemorial, the eastern part of Jerusalem has symbolized its spiritual aspect, whereas the western part signifies its new dimension as the capital of Israel. Topographically, both centres are stages, two natural amphitheaters situated on either side of a watershed. One has a view to the Judean Desert; the other, facing west, overlooks the National Precinct. The Supreme Court Building is the focal point of the National Precinct and will become its keystone. The building's spatial alignment toward the east is intended to strengthen and accentuate the affinity between the two amphitheaters. Thus the structure forms a link in a chain of buildings and sites leading from the Rockefeller Museum, extending through the Damascus Gate, the Russian Compound, Zion Square, the Ben Yehuda Mall, and proceeding to Kiryat Ben-Gurion. The design takes into account an additional axis, the ridge (divide) connecting the gateway to the city with the Convention Centre, the Supreme Court, the Knesset and The Israel Museum. This axis bisects the Supreme Court lengthwise, through its centre.

"These axes have created an internal, urban dimension which divides the complex into four disparate components. The relationship between the private and the public aspects within, is one of affinity and confrontation. In the strife between concept and form, the public space creates a balance among the different sections, while preserving the identity of each.

* Concept 12 included all the ingredients of the final scheme, some of which were slightly modifed in alternatives 13-16.

Akin to the cardinal axes of Roman camps, the 'Cardo' and the 'Decumanus' carve out the quarters of the Old City, thus partitioning and delineating them. Each zealously guards its identity, and yet the teeming activity within produces a living connection, a meeting place where differences melt away. The same principle has been applied to the Supreme Court Building: the entrance placed at the intersection of the east-west and north-south axes both determines the areas of partition and interweaves a texture of interrelations between its parts.

"From the outset, we allowed the two axes to divide the courthouse into four sections: the library, the judges' chambers, the courtrooms and the parking area. Each part, with a 'will of its own,' sought to upstage the others, almost with the same tenacity with which various Christian sects vies for territory in the Church of the Holy Sepulchre.

"After working out alternative schemes, with each of the building's various parts beginning to assume its final form, we had our main characters – but as yet no performance. We had to uncover the link between the different personalities and forge them into a cohesive family. In looking for a common denominator, we returned to the intersection. This is the internalized point around which the building evolves, whose force gave birth to the massive stone wall that bisects the courthouse from east to west, and in so doing makes peace among the four contenders.

"The subdivision into sections was clear, but the large masonry wall, a continuous presence throughout the building, created a new order. As the wall rose, the internal complexity of the building took over, defying its initial simple partition and becoming an experience in itself. With the vertical layering of the building which defined the public, the judges' and the prisoners' levels – each an independent, horizontal plane – the order became even more intricate.

"The competition programme was based on a pragmatic approach tending to translate the building components into quantitative terms. Programmes of this nature rely on a purely utilitarian perception which, in the name of functional architecture, seeks to create an efficient, mechanistic structure.

Section of church mosaic from Madaba (in Jordan), showing the Cardo maximus of Jerusalem (Sixth Century C.E.)

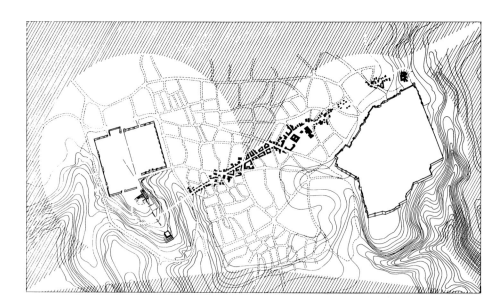

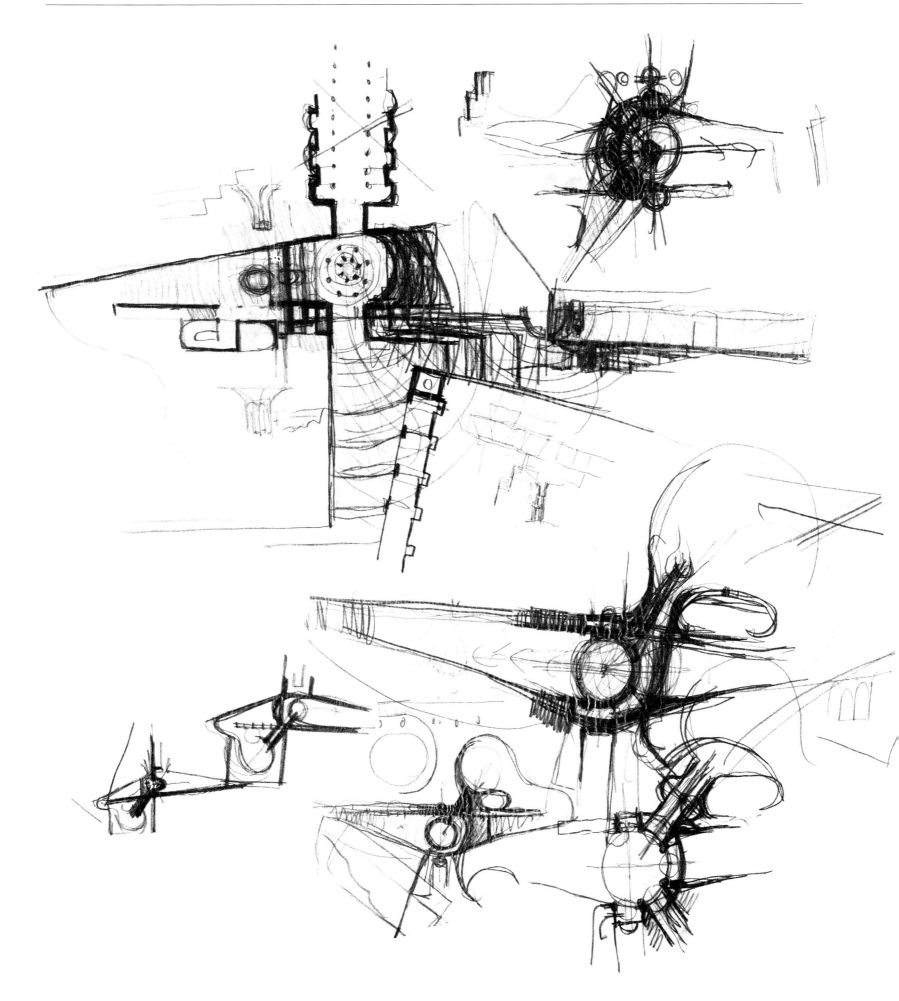

"The formula commonly used to check a building's viability is the multiple of gross (net + tare) area by construction costs per square meter. Net areas can be precisely estimated, as these are the spaces allotted to the building's permanent users, in this instance: the judges, the administration which they oversee, and other services. Net areas are calculated on the basis of the nature of the designated activity, position in the internal hierarchy and place in the building's functional system. It is always possible to define and measure each work-station according to the space required. Only the public dimension of the building defies scientific quantification. That is why in the architectural programme public spaces are present in the tare areas, which also include corridors, stairwells and conveniences – the areas essential for maintaining and servicing the net areas.

"The competition programme did not take any position regarding the public dimension, leaving it to our discretion. The tare areas, therefore, included the representative public spaces, expressing the social and cultural order without which there can be no public building. The public dimension affects and determines the structure's architectural image. This is of the utmost importance, particularly in buildings in which the public spends long hours, sometimes in tense anticipation. This aspect – which, as a rule, programmes conspicuously overlook – answers the question: Will the public be able to spend its time there in a cultured and appropriate atmosphere?

"The unique character of each building reflects the abstract ideas behind it. We searched for this identity from the start and continued to pursue it throughout the entire design process. Here all our senses came into play as we attempted to measure those elements which can be measured, to sense that which can be felt, to love that which can be loved and, finally, to behold that which can be seen...

"The path leading to the public dimension is often strewn with surprises. Even though the building does not have particularly large public areas (certainly not the largest of those included in some of the entries), we began to reduce them after the competition, in compliance with the Court's request. That is to say, we began to fill the open, tare areas of the public level with the net functions originally intended for the floor above it.

"The administration was moved up to the public level while the library and courtrooms were moved down. Stage after stage, the pattern of circulation within the building was stabilized: the public steps directly into the courtrooms, the judges descend into the courtrooms and the prisoners ascend from below. Although the public level had been totally transformed, footsteps still fade away and vanish, as in the large foyer (salle des pas perdues) of Paris' supreme court building."

Sketches of building layouts with access from the west

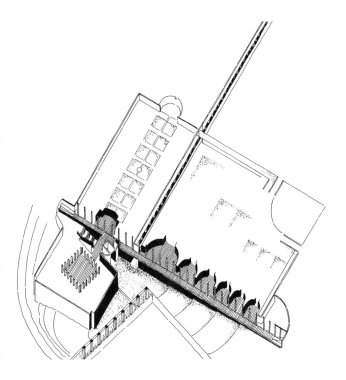

Entrance level

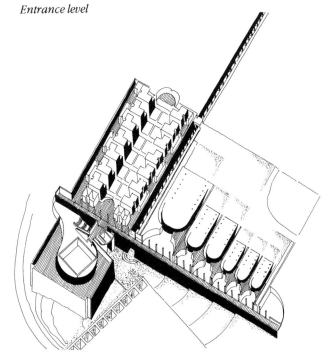

Judges' level

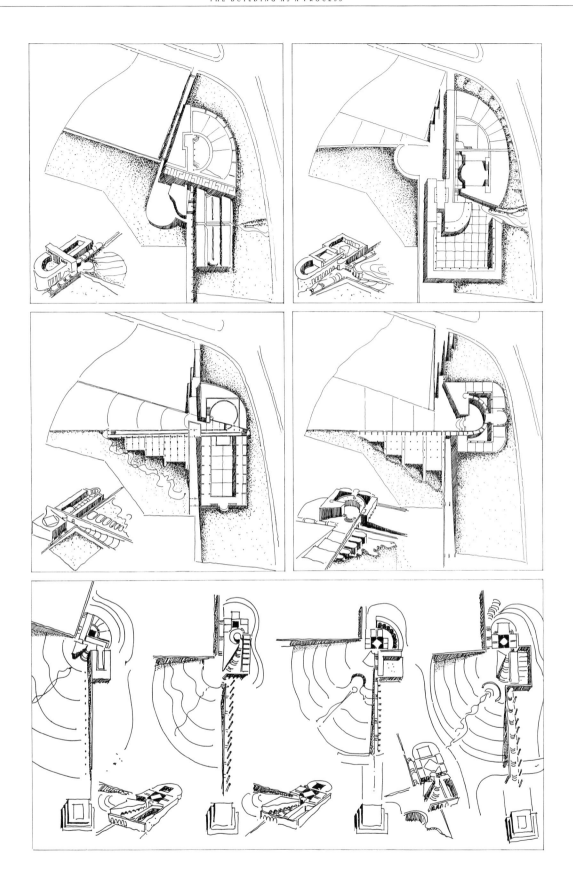

Early layout schemes

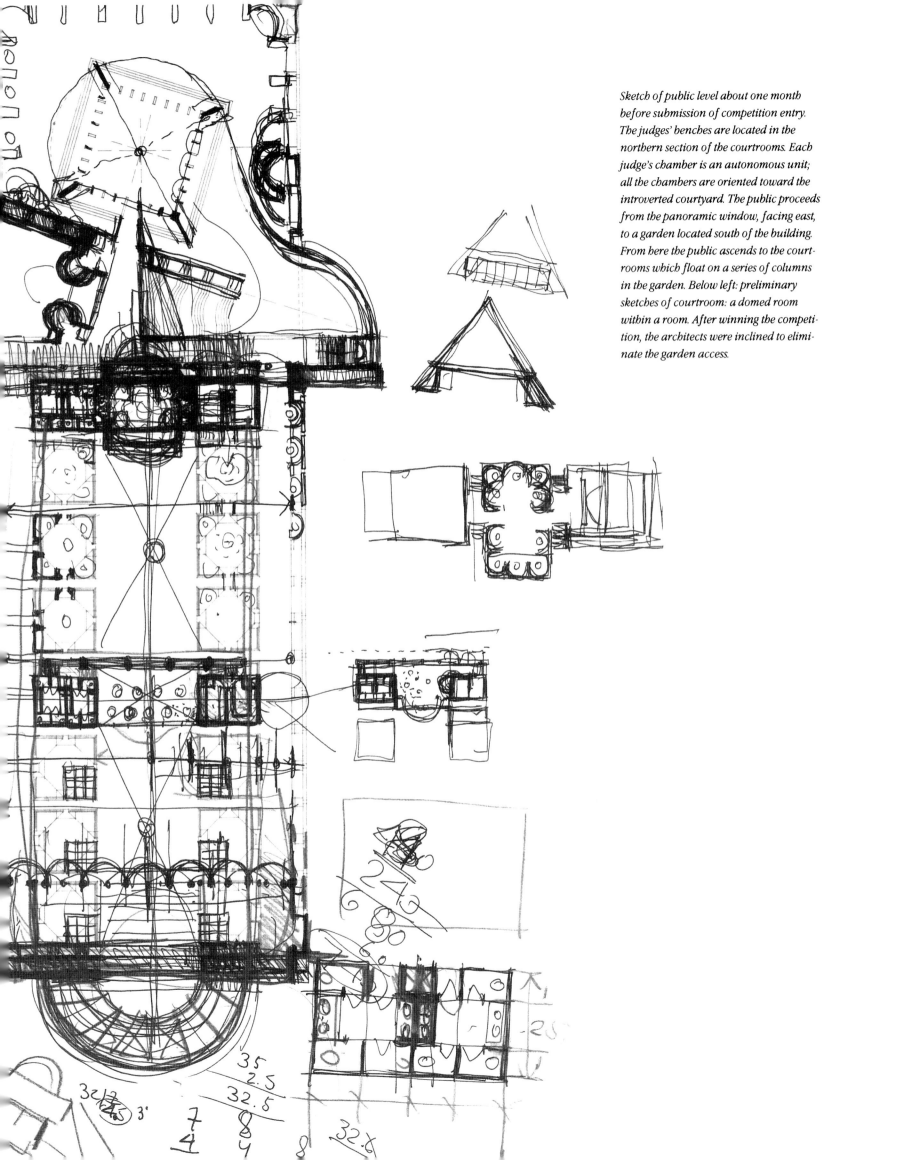

Sketch of public level about one month before submission of competition entry. The judges' benches are located in the northern section of the courtrooms. Each judge's chamber is an autonomous unit; all the chambers are oriented toward the introverted courtyard. The public proceeds from the panoramic window, facing east, to a garden located south of the building. From here the public ascends to the courtrooms which float on a series of columns in the garden. Below left: preliminary sketches of courtroom: a domed room within a room. After winning the competition, the architects were inclined to eliminate the garden access.

Early sketch of entrance and pyramid

Alternative 1

The entrance to the Supreme Court Building is from the west, through the Knesset axis, and leads to the Grand Foyer, which is delineated by the courtrooms. To the east, opposite the entrance, the foyer terminates in a large panoramic window overlooking Jerusalem and Sacher Park. An administration wing extends from either side of the entrance. The library faces the foyer, encircling it. The judges' level, directly above, delineates the library. Its presence is prominent in the space within and dominates the Sacher Garden from without. Here the architectural composition consists of three distinct parts: Judges' Courtyard and Administration, courtrooms and parking area. The courtrooms are disposed like a fan, facing the Rose Garden to the south-west.

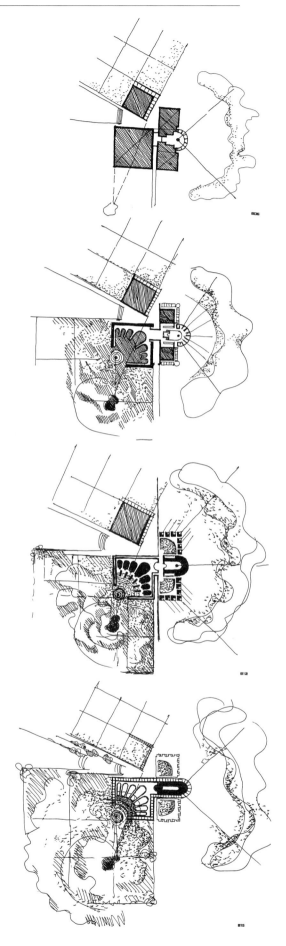

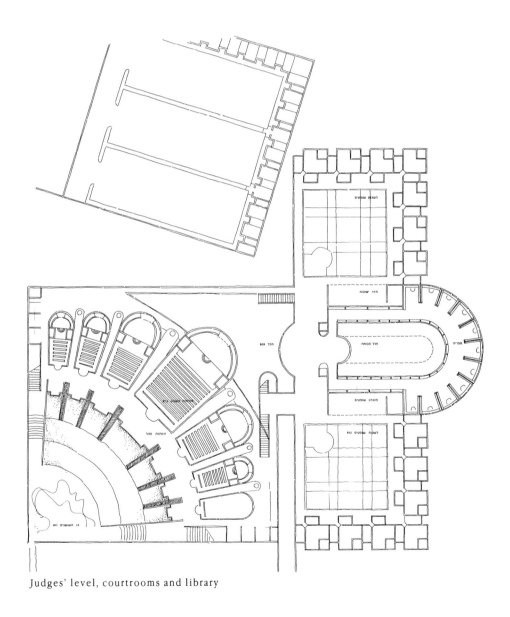

Judges' level, courtrooms and library

Alternative 2

The entrance is from the north, parallel to the Knesset axis. An introverted, central foyer is circumscribed by the administration wing. The judges' chambers overhead are displayed at the perimeter of the Courtyard and open out to Sacher Park and Jerusalem. The library is situated at the centre of the Judges' Courtyard and serves as a threshold to the courtrooms. These are disposed along the foyer, which terminates in a window facing west. The courtrooms look out on a park which is a direct extension of the Rose Garden. This composition consists of three distinct parts: judges' chambers and Administration, courtrooms, parking area.

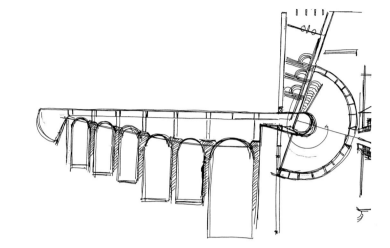

Entrance and public level

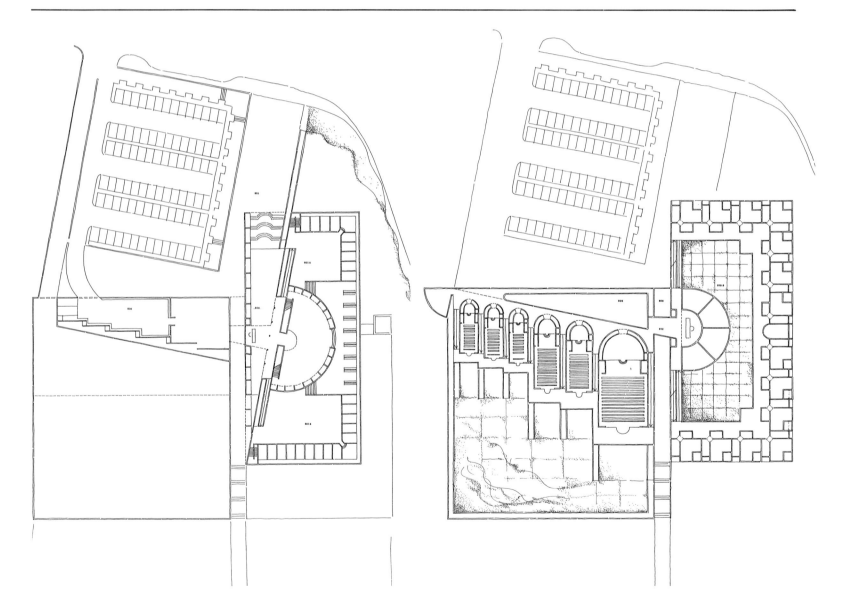

Public entrance level and Administration

Courtroom level and judges' wing

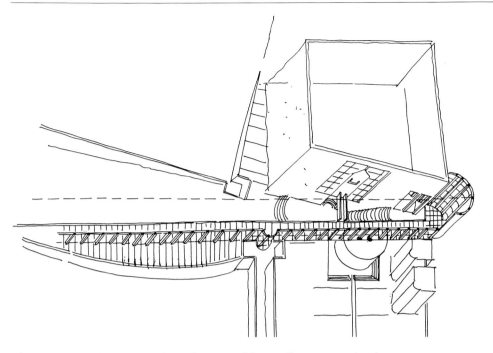

Alternative 3

The entrance is from the east. At the intersection of the north-south and east-west axes, the public proceeds eastward towards the main entrance and the grand foyer overlooking Sacher Park and Jerusalem. This disengages the foyer and library, making them a free-standing object, connected to the rest of the building via a perpendicular bridge. The geometric inclination of the foyer, and the pyramid within it, express the desire to include this section (like the parking area) in the geometric urban order, rather than aligned with the Knesset.

The entrance to the building from the east is like an alley open to the sky

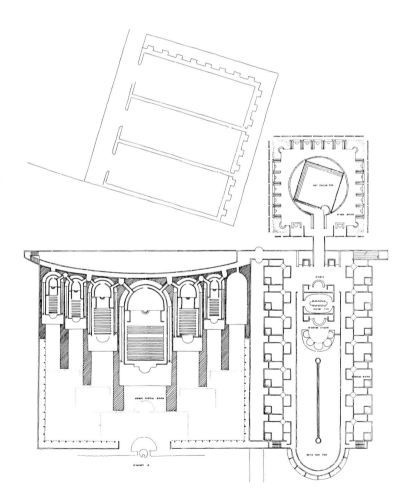

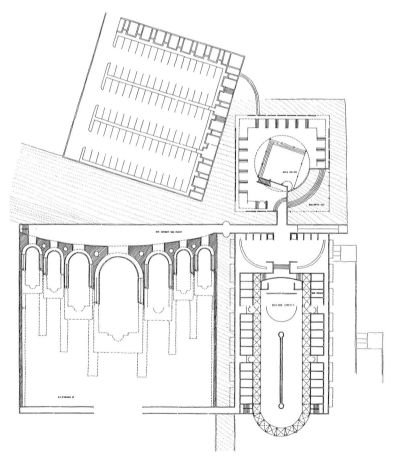

Judges' chambers level, library and courtrooms

Public level and Administration

45

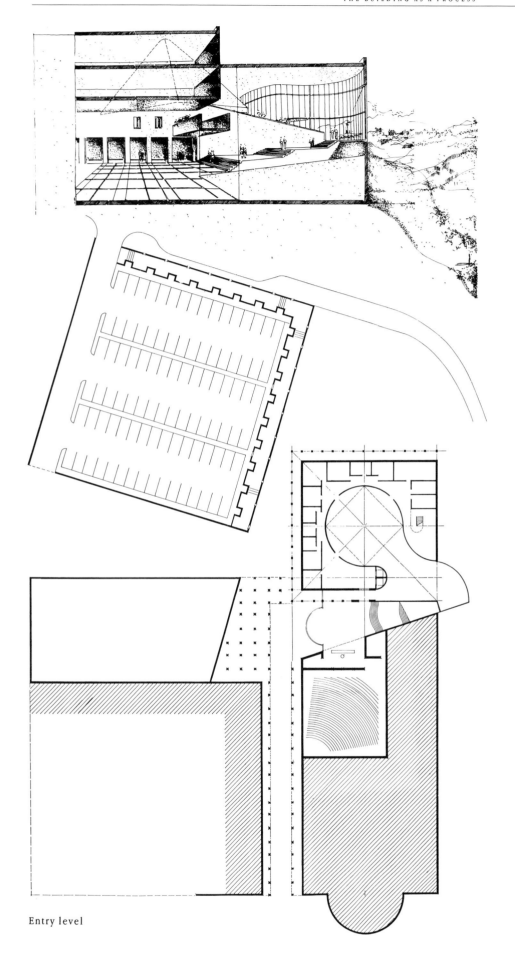

Entry level

Alternative 4a

The arcade along the Knesset axis presses north-ward, circumscribing the library wing and Administration. The library and the pyramid space, at its centre, are set along the Knesset axis, with the geometric deflection remaining only in the parking area. Administrative functions are carried out at ground level, separating the cermonial part of the building from the day-to-day functional one.

Alternative 4b

The arcade along the Knesset axis presses north-
ward, circumscribing the library wing. Entry is
via a covered, colonnaded square. The Administration has now been finalized one level overhead. Pedestrian movement is in one of two
directions: towards the courtrooms or to the
Administration, once again overlooking the
square before disappearing into the various
wings.

The circulation pattern splits into two. There are
two bridges: one leading to the Administration,
the other to the courtrooms.

Axonometric of the public level

Alternative 5

The judges' chambers are disposed along a peripheral corridor overlooking the Judges' Court-yard, which widens out at the entrance to each chamber. The articled clerks enter their rooms through the secretarial space. Each chamber has a patio which frames the outside view and diffuses the light entering the chambers.

The entry and the spatial sequence around it have been finalized. The entrance, shielded by the courtrooms, is now from the west. A glass wall begins with a panoramic window overlooking the city and penetrates the building as it embraces the pyramid and delineates the library, located one story above the entrance level. The judges' chambers, which were previously introverted and overlooked the courtyard, now command a view of the Jerusalem landscape.

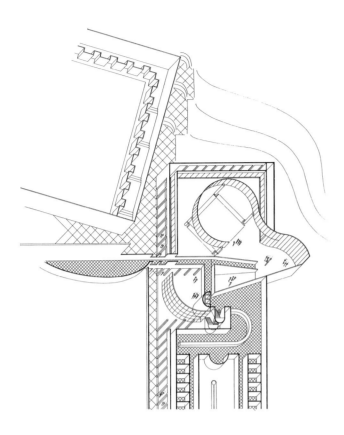

Ground level plan – the entrance space is protected by the courtrooms

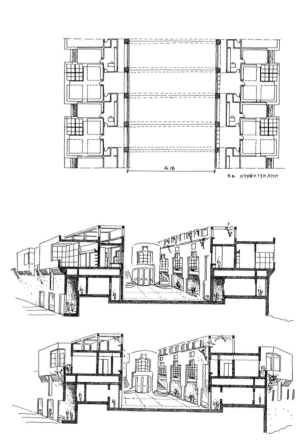

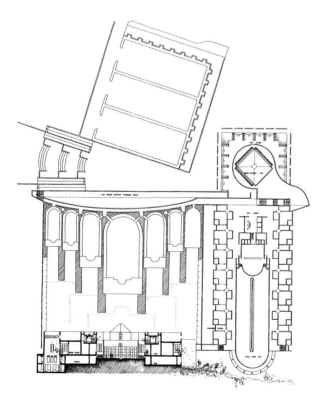

Plan and section of judges' level

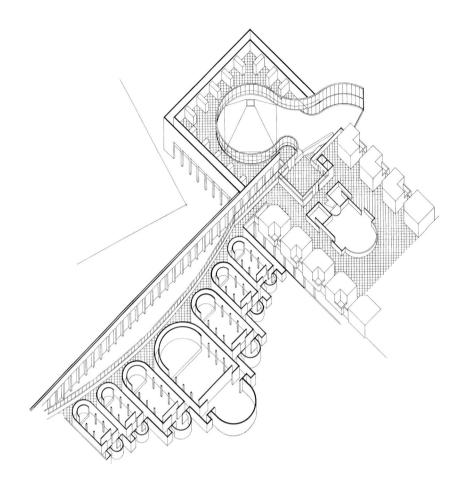

Axonometric of the judges' level

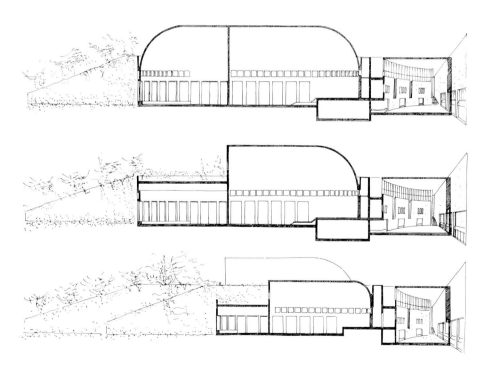

Detailed sections of courtrooms

Alternative 6

The waiting areas below the 'floating' courtrooms have been eliminated. The courtrooms are now situated on ground level. The public ascends to the courtrooms, the judges descend. The public waiting areas overlook the Wohl Rose Garden. The glass wall, beginning at the panoramic window, swings around the pyramid as it extends in a circular pattern along the stone wall and terminates in a window facing west. The glass curtain is disposed in a circular pattern; the stone wall proceeds in a straight line.

Section through courtrooms

Public entrance to courtrooms – the glass wall, beginning at the panoramic window, follows the contours of the courtroom wing

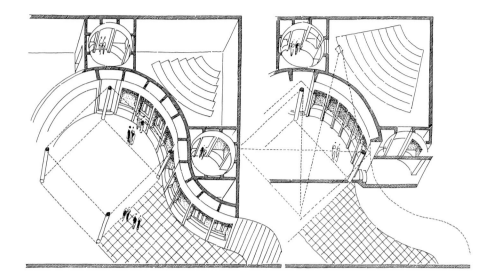

Alternative 7

The colonnaded level below the library is now replete with functions, including a lecture hall and advocates' rooms. Showcases are included in the thick curved wall encircling the pyramid. The wall is a divider between the public and the stacks. It shields the entrance space, making it even more introverted, as though it were wrapped up in itself.

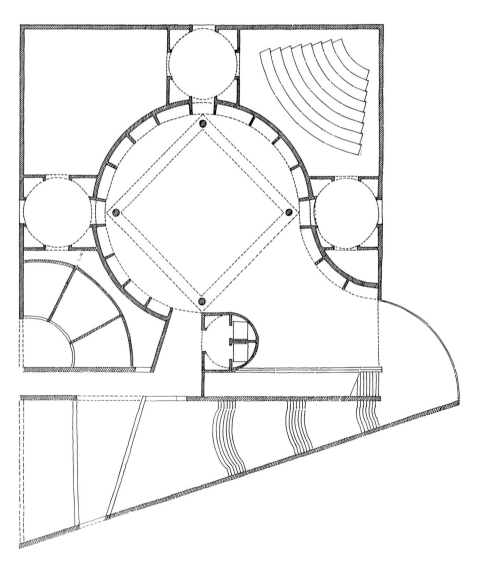

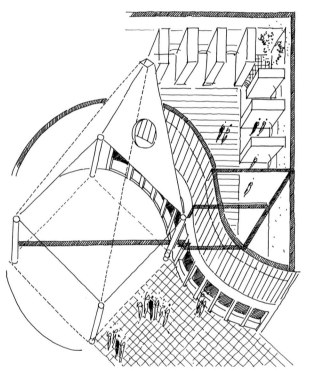

The three-tiered library has been moved to the public level. The main floor is accessible to the public; the two top storeys are reserved for judges' use. The three storeys recede vertically, forming a valley of books which takes up the entire pyramid space.

President's level
Judges' level, library
Public level
Engine room and shelter

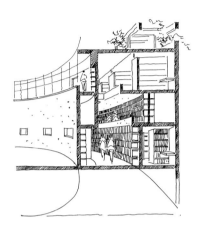

Double wall separating the library from the entrance

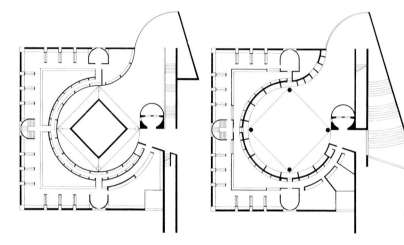

Plan public level   Plan judges' level

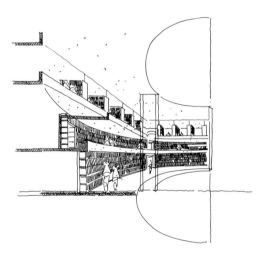

Section through library and entrance loggia

View of library from entrance

Alternative 8

The courtrooms have been restored to their original location and the public is crowded into an elongated, narrow foyer which gradually expands as it approaches the large courtroom at its centre. It is terminated by a cafeteria opening out to the Wohl Rose Garden. An attempt has been made to link the judges' chambers with the walled garden via a bridge facing the Knesset.

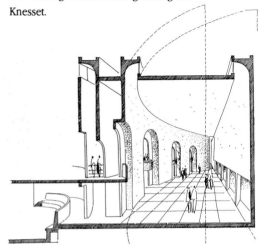

Section through foyer and waiting area beneath large courtroom

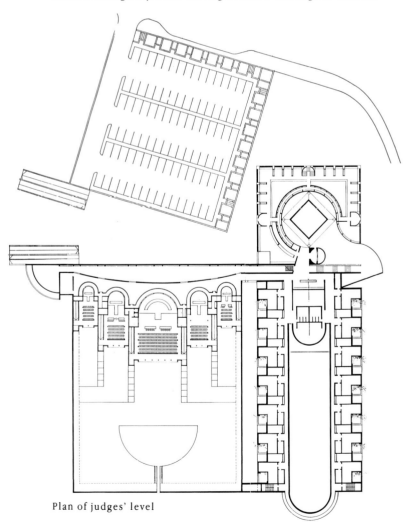

Plan of judges' level

Alternative 9

The foyer has been rotated 180° and now faces west – in the direction of the Rose Garden. The public enters the courtrooms via a foyer that widens out towards, and merges with, the walled garden. The courtrooms are perpendicular to the Knesset axis, shortening the distance from the judges' chambers. The judges enter from either end of the courtroom wing. The judges' chambers now face west and no longer view the city.

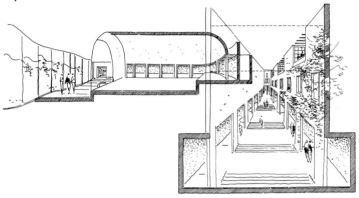

Section through Knesset route and courtrooms

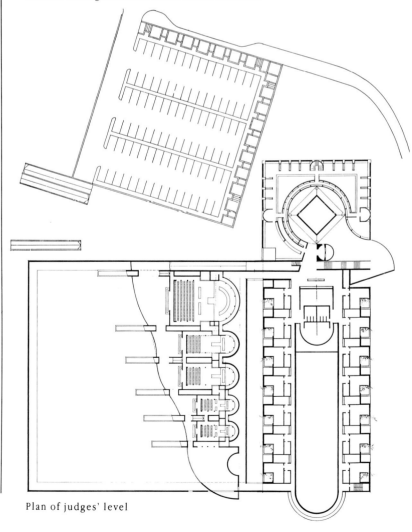

Plan of judges' level

Alternative 10

The courtrooms have been moved to ground level and are arranged in a semi-circle within the garden. They are grouped like a family, whose centre is the inner courtyard, open to the sky. The public proceeds through the introverted arcades towards the courtrooms, from which it is possible to reach the walled garden.

Plan of judges' level

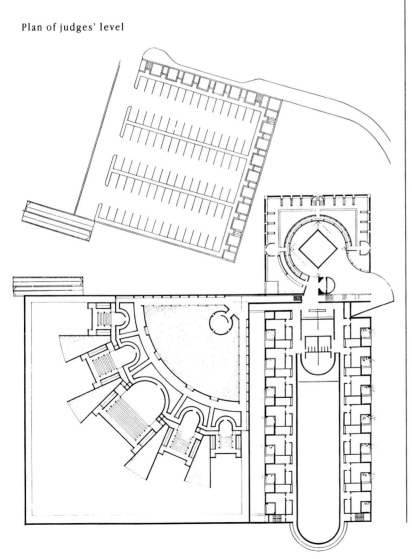

Alternative 11

The courtrooms are disposed along a diagonal axis which bisects the courtyard. The public waits in the 'loggia' and step directly into the courtooms. At either end of the foyer there is a passage to the courtroom garden located to the south, with a cafeteria at the tip.

Entry level plan

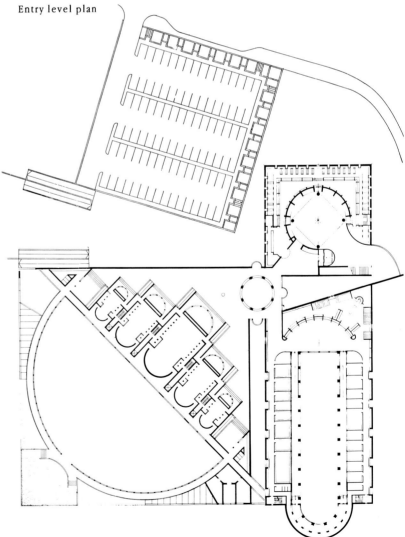

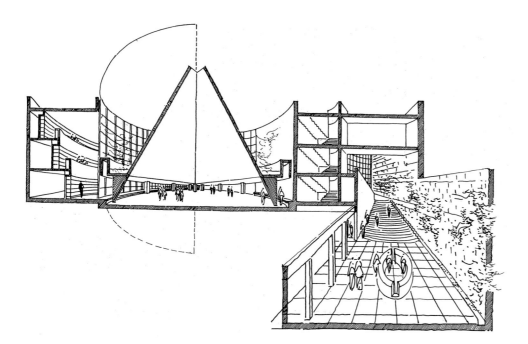

Section through main entrance and library

Alternative 12

The final version, which served as a basis for the construction and bid documents. The public ascends to the courtrooms, the judges descend. Beneath the large courtroom, there is a cafeteria which opens out towards the Wohl Rose Garden and is accessible from the foyer. The large stone wall is not yet a continuous whole. Here it is split close to the intersection of the axes, and is accentuated by columns bearing the load of the large conference room above.

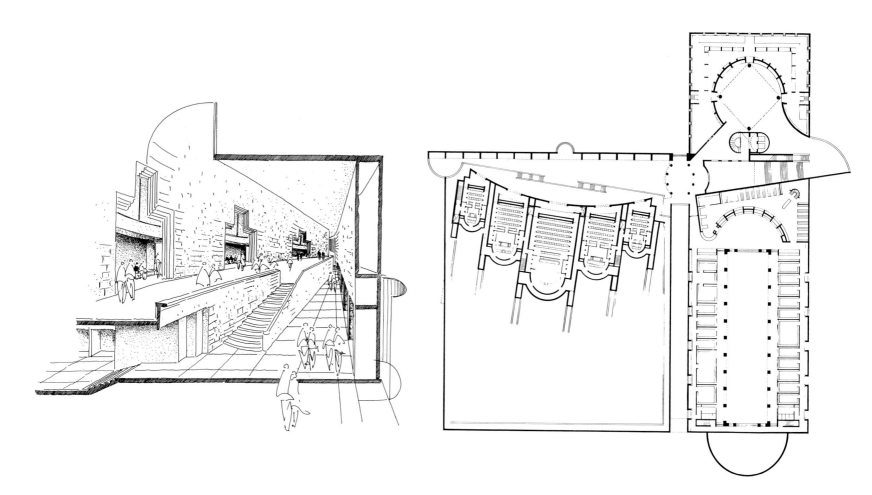

Section through foyer and cafeteria showing ascent to courtrooms

Grand foyer level plan and Administration

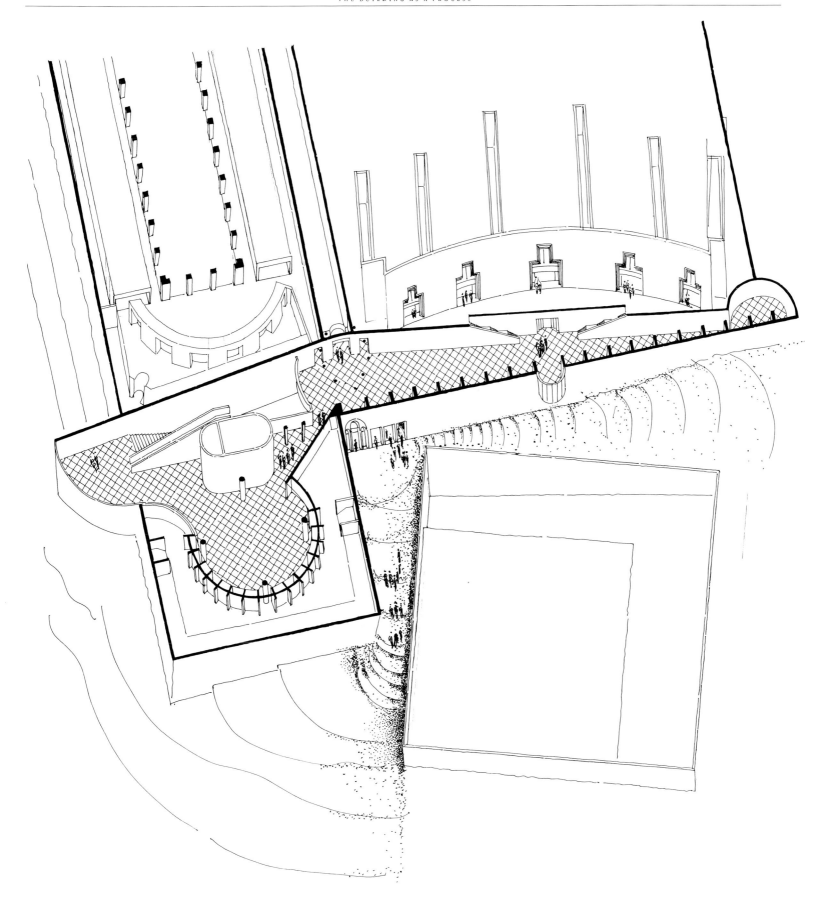

Axonometric of the large stone wall before it became bow-shaped and continuous

THE PLANNING TEAM

*A*fter winning the competition, the architects held biweekly meetings over a two-year period, with Yad Hanadiv, the client, and with justices of the Supreme Court. The architects studied the workings of the Court at close hand; Yad Hanadiv and the judges, in turn, reviewed the architectural plans in depth.

In the course of the ongoing dialogue, it was decided that the responsibility for budget and initial cost estimates would devolve on Dan Wind. Eliezer Rahat was the engineer appointed by Yad Hanadiv to supervise the final design and budget and to implement the project. Karmi-Melamede and Karmi were given a free hand in seeking solutions to specific problems, provided they did not deviate from their basic concepts. In reviewing the building process one might say that each party was somewhat in the position of a ruler who, like the ideal Biblical king,[1] should not abuse his power; no one could exercise unrestrained authority.

Once the architectural plans had been approved by the client and the various authorities, there remained much to do. Although the overall design was well advanced, design and construction of the technical systems were just beginning. Rahat suggested to the architects and to Yad Hanadiv that work be allowed to proceed according to the fast-track method (planning carried out simultaneously with construction) in order to keep to both timetable and budget.

In 1989, Rahat issued a tender on the basis of the existing plans. During the casting of the skeleton, designed and calculated by Dr. Eliyahu Traum, the architects developed working drawings for implementation. Rahat and Yad Hanadiv reviewed the detailed drawings. This 'modus operandi' forced the technical consultants (electricity, plumbing, air-conditioning, etc.) and the architects into a tight work schedule; the pace of planning was in fact dictated by progress on the site.

From 1990, most working sessions were held in Rahat's office at the construction site. The architects came to Jerusalem once a week to monitor the construction. They commented, made proposals and occasionally asked for changes.

The planning team became as one family, united in the desire to achieve high-quality in both design and implementation. Rahat's involvement (together with that of the project architects from Karmi Architects, Ltd., Tel Aviv: project supervisor Meir Drezner, senior architects Iftach Issacharov, Simone Friedman, and architects Alan Aranoff, Daniel Azerrad, Ruth Rotholz-Van Eck, Motty Shyovitz and Rami Yogev) influenced the nature of the decisions. The architects resolved to use local materials: white stone from Mitzpe Ramon, crust-stone from all across the country, Atzmon and Vered Hagalil stone for flooring, as well as plain plaster and bush-hammered concrete. In order to highlight the natural beauty of the material, they made certain that a high level of craftsmanship was maintained, paying close attention to the smallest particulars. The

North elevation: view of parking area and entrance. Upon entering, the public 'bisects' the visible Knesset axis. The Wohl Rose Garden is situated to the south; Government ministries and the Israel Museum are to the right.

architects' meticulous detailing often required Rahat to exercise his powers of persuasion with Yad Hanadiv. According to the architects, "Eliezer was the client's emissary, but he considered himself first and foremost the spokesman of the building's architecture. Even when he pushed for compromise, it was carried out in the spirit of our intentions, of what we wanted, in order that the building receive its just due...."

In the final analysis, the fast track resulted in savings: dry construction spared time and expense, despite the high cost of certain components. The building's success may be attributed in large measure to Rahat's technical know-how and his successful management of budget and timetable. Overall costs proved lower than projected by Yad Hanadiv and the building was turned over to the Supreme Court almost on schedule. (Construction was held up by barely three months owing to the Gulf War, which erupted in January 1991, the resulting situation in the territories and the unusually severe winter of 1992).

1. Deuteronomy 17:16-17.

Aerial photograph from the south, showing the ensconced Supreme Court Building, bisected by the ridge (Knesset axis). The judges' chambers are to the right, the court-rooms are located to the left, the Hilton Hotel and Binyaney Ha'ooma are to the north.

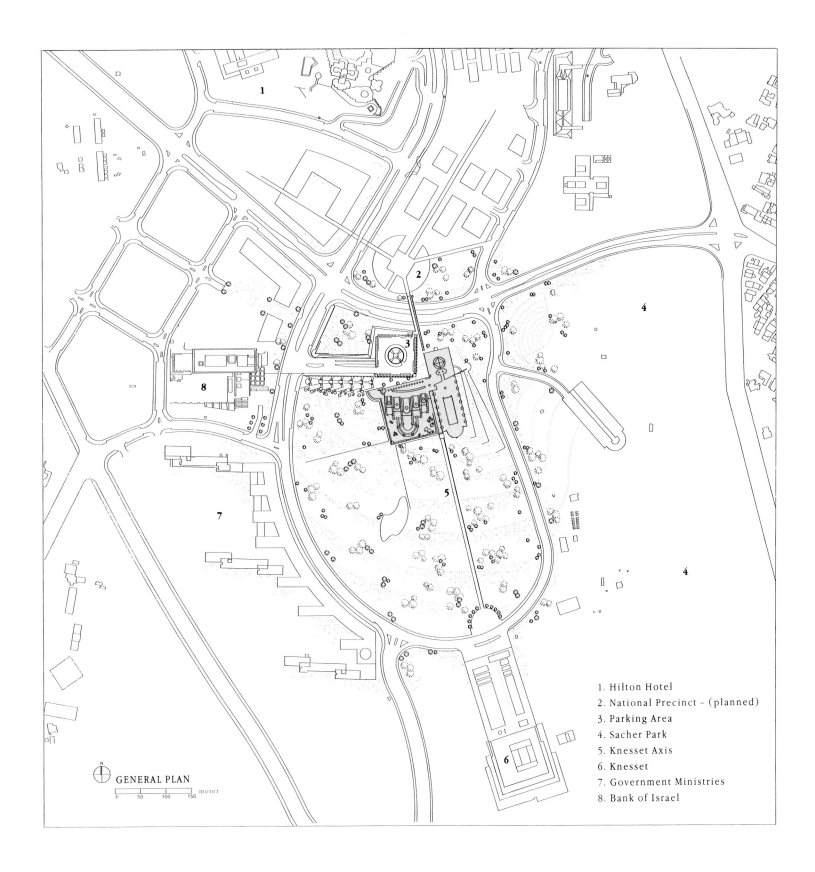

1. Hilton Hotel
2. National Precinct - (planned)
3. Parking Area
4. Sacher Park
5. Knesset Axis
6. Knesset
7. Government Ministries
8. Bank of Israel

GENERAL PLAN

meter
0   50   100   150

Layout of the National Precinct showing Supreme Court Building at the centre of a natural amphitheater. To the east, the building overlooks the slopes of Sacher Park and the Nahla'ot and Mahaneh Yehuda neighbourhoods; to the west – the Bank of Israel and several Government ministries. According to the architects' urban concept, the building is sited at the centre of a grid which accentuates the northern ridge (north-south axis). The axis running from the entry to the Knesset Plaza bisects the building. Once a bridge is erected over the highway to the north of the building, the main entry will be from this direction. At present the main approach by public transportation is from the west.

Aerial photograph of Supreme Court Building from the west

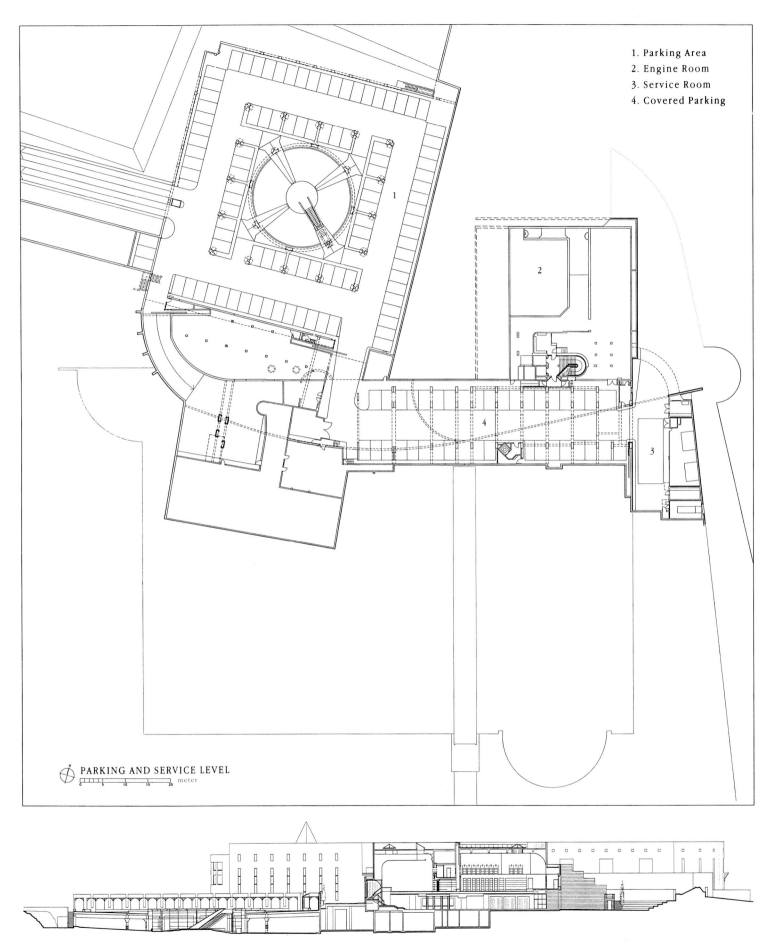

1. Parking Area
2. Engine Room
3. Service Room
4. Covered Parking

PARKING AND SERVICE LEVEL

0 5 10 15 20
meter

North-south section through the large courtroom and parking area

61

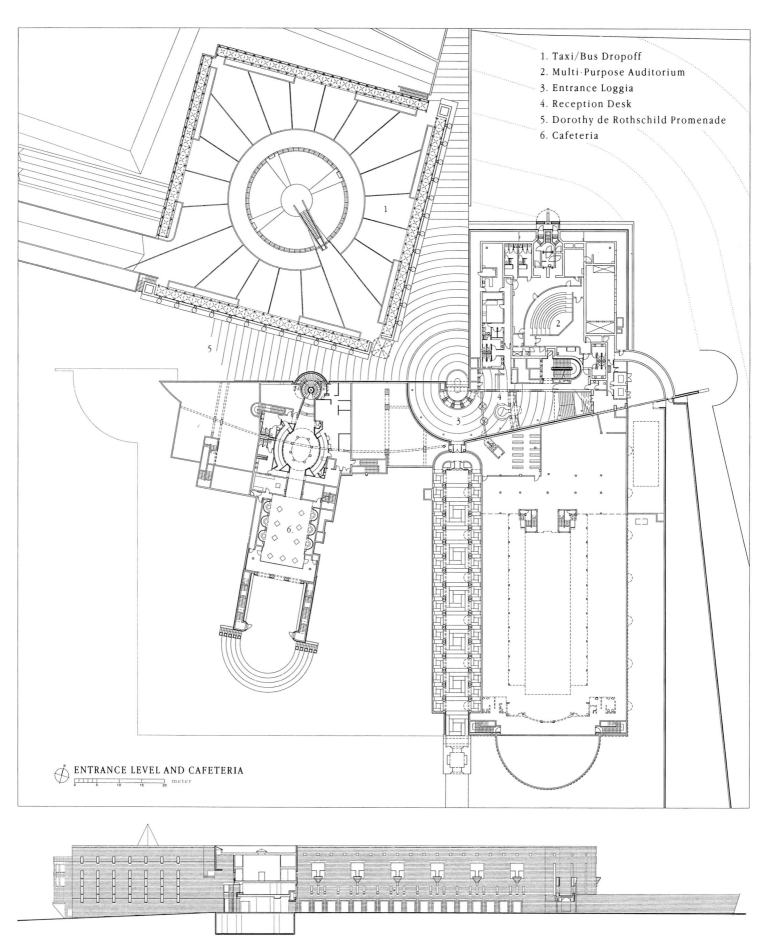

1. Taxi/Bus Dropoff
2. Multi-Purpose Auditorium
3. Entrance Loggia
4. Reception Desk
5. Dorothy de Rothschild Promenade
6. Cafeteria

ENTRANCE LEVEL AND CAFETERIA

North-south section through Knesset route

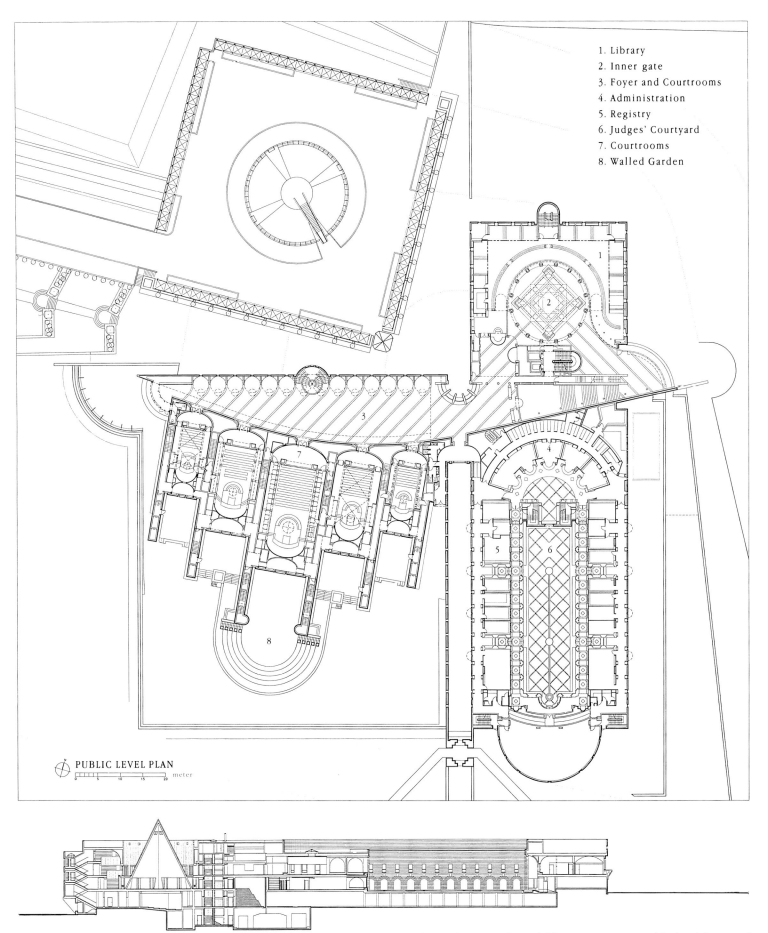

1. Library
2. Inner gate
3. Foyer and Courtrooms
4. Administration
5. Registry
6. Judges' Courtyard
7. Courtrooms
8. Walled Garden

PUBLIC LEVEL PLAN

meter
0   5   10   15   20

North-south section through library, inner gate and Judges' Courtyard

63

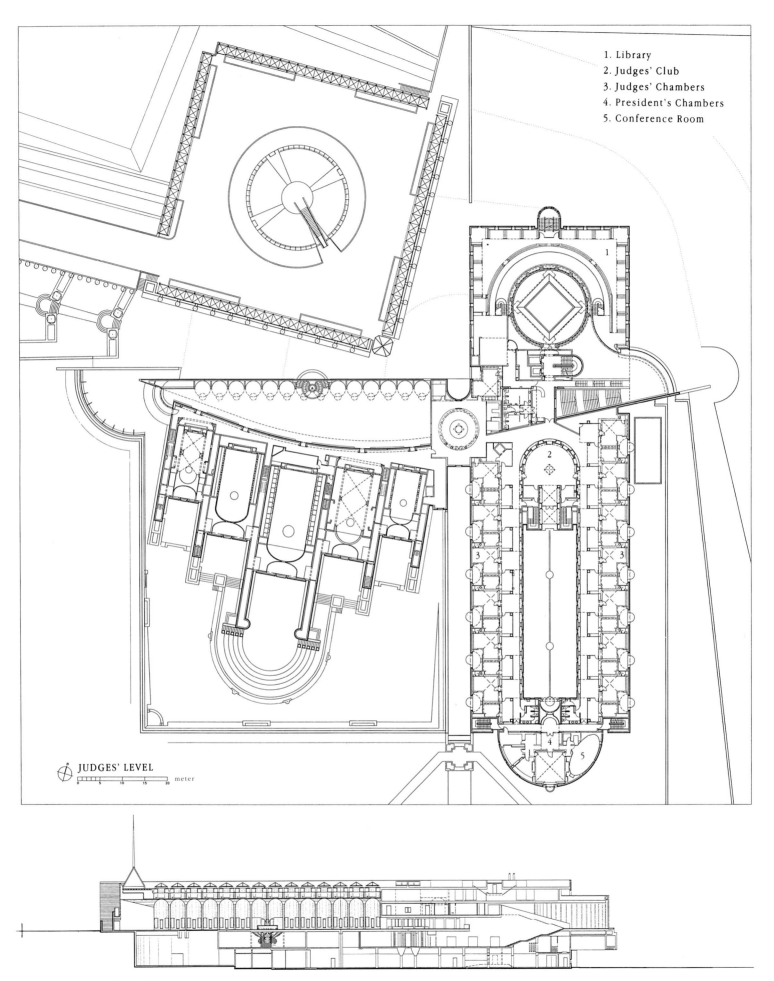

1. Library
2. Judges' Club
3. Judges' Chambers
4. President's Chambers
5. Conference Room

JUDGES' LEVEL

0 5 10 15 20 meter

East-west section through foyer

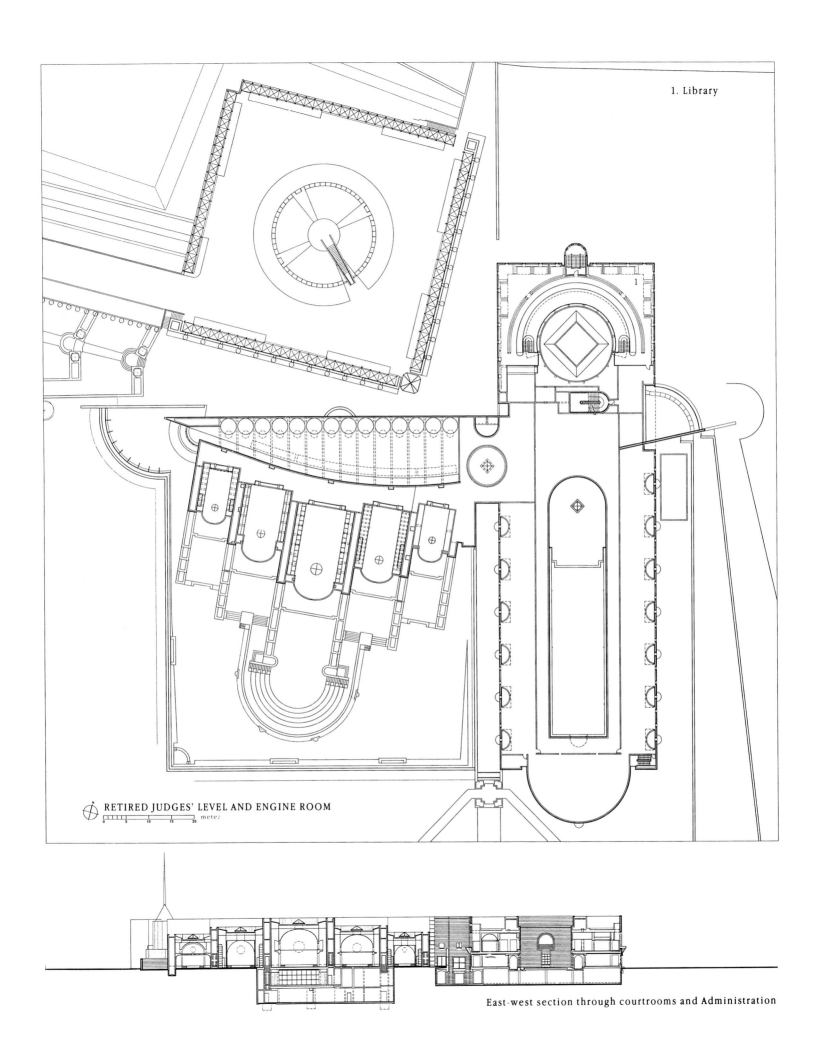

1. Library

RETIRED JUDGES' LEVEL AND ENGINE ROOM

East-west section through courtrooms and Administration

65

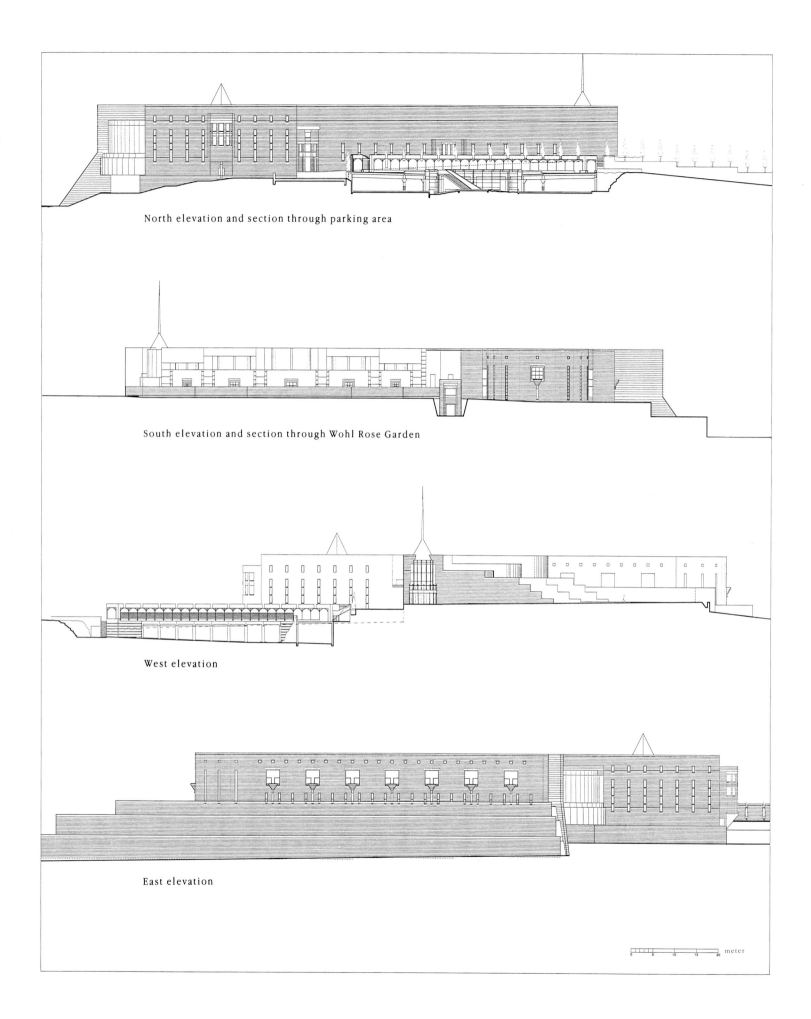

North elevation and section through parking area

South elevation and section through Wohl Rose Garden

West elevation

East elevation

meter

Aerial view of the National Precinct

South elevation: courtrooms nestling in the hill

Cascading wall linking the building to the garden

Dorothy de Rothschild Promenade

Window facing west

North and east elevations

Library stairwell protruding to the north

View of entry from the north

THE ENTRANCE

Although the building does not have an imposing entrance, it is designed to receive throngs of visitors. The overall area is large, even relative to the great number of people who enter its halls. Intended to be commensurate with the unquestionable stature of Israel's Supreme Court, the building does not require an overwhelming or ostentatious presence.

Neither the location of the entrance nor the approach to it is obtrusive. From afar, the portal projects moderate strength and authority – owing partly to the fact that it is not centered on a symmetrical front. Conspicuously absent are steep steps leading to the entrance – a conventional symbol of authority. The portal has been placed, as though by chance, at the junction of the building's four sections (library, courtrooms, judges' chambers and parking area). It is an integral part of the structure, while cautioning against undue manifestations of splendor.

Only as one nears the gateway does this feeling subside; its height is indeed impressive. Some may consider that they are worthy of passing through. To others, the scriptural verse "and we were in our own sight as grasshoppers" (Numbers 13:33) will come to mind. There will also be those who will maintain that the feeling of insignificance is but a small price to pay for the reverence accorded the rule of law.

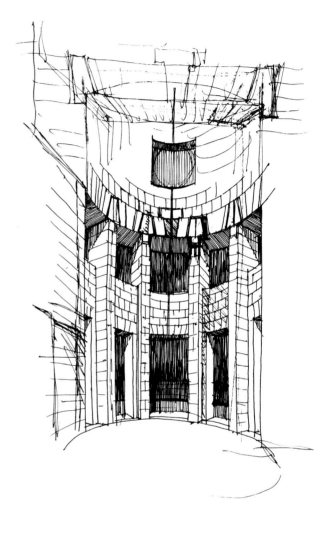

The vertical contours of the gate are meant to reflect the Court's aspirations towards hierarchy, while bearing in mind that here all are equal. This may account for the architects' decision to accord the building an archaic scale. The height of the portal, they contended, "does not express hierarchy but rather the building's egalitarian thrust." That is the rationale for the double reading of the threshold, a ceremonial height of three storeys, revealing the barest hint of the building's interior, articulated by the one-story functional opening of the entry.

One enters a wide space. What appears from the outside to be a narrow entry able to accommodate only a few people at a time, widens, taking on the dimensions of a loggia. Once inside, the architectural concept is evident: the portal has been erected at the junction of two axes. The first is that of the Knesset, which the gateway overlooks, as it opens on an arcade leading to the Knesset Plaza. The gate's role and location are emphasized vertically, exploiting the high ground. If the Knesset axis acts as the 'Cardo' of the structure, then the intersecting axis (one story above the entrance), leading towards the city to the east and directing the eye toward the Mediterranean Sea to the west, may be considered the 'Decumanus.'

Beyond its relationship to the other structures within view, the entrance is the focus of a new spatial setting. The building symbolizes the rule of Law. Its relatively elevated location transforms the entrance into a 'threshold' to the National Precinct, the area which includes the Knesset, the Prime Minister's office, many ministries and the

Bank of Israel. A sense of expansiveness is generated, the feeling that no key could possibly fit this gateway.

The Supreme Court Building was designed to express the precise opposite of "turning aside the needy from justice" or "taking away the right from the poor" (Isaiah 10:2). One may question whether a building can at one and the same time express both the moral authority of a court of law and its supreme power. In the absence of an unequivocal solution to this dilemma, the pristine character of the entrance has been stressed; it is like an opening hewn into the wall. Its primoridal character conveys the idea that where law and justice are concerned, there can be no carry-over of purported prior authority; the Supreme Court Building is not competing with Solomon's Temple, Greek temples or traditional synagogues. But innovativeness does not imply the abrogation of majesty and stature.

To the gallery of Jerusalem gateways – the YMCA gate, the Old City's Damascus and Jaffa Gates – has been added this original doorway, which, although evoking a Jerusalem archetype, does not display the traditional arched form. Indirectly, this architectural resolution makes us contemplate our national culture, the choice between traditional metaphors and their expression in a new language, liberated from the past.

After entering, one ascends a flight of stone stairs alongside the massive wall. The wall is a continuous element extending across the building. Dry construction was used in the cladding, leaving the stone unmarked by craftsmen's hands. The wall evokes a primeval desert mood, while instilling a formal and ceremonial atmosphere.

The high ceiling here generates the odd feeling that one has been whisked up from down below, surfacing into the light of day. A window facing east admits a vista of Jerusalem ("a city of red roof tiles," according to Karmi-Melamede), of the Nahla'ot and Mahane Yehuda neighbourhoods. Here the large stone wall breaks free of the building and continues eastward, as if it were a fragment of an older, larger structure.

Looking to the left of the panoramic window, one can see a section of the foyer, but neither the opening to it nor the entrances to the courtrooms. The break-up of the ground level public space is most striking here. The visitor is introduced to an architectural gambit. Looking away from the window, to the building, although clearly within the courthouse, one seems to be searching for something. Unable to perceive the space in its totality, one is forced to realize the architectural metaphor of the building by walking. This is a court of one's own, a path personally travelled.

Turning from the large window, one experiences a momentary doubt: where am I heading? The eye, far swifter than the foot, hesitates, bewildered. Perhaps there is an instant of 'alienation,' and, at the same time, of reflection. This is a turning point: either one retraces one's footsteps and exits, or one begins, like the space itself, to move toward the courtrooms. This is a fine architectural interpretation of monumentality, avoiding the familiar centrally oriented space which dwarfs or dominates the individual.

Above: *arcade of flat arches along the Knesset route*

Right: *Patios of judges' chambers and wall enclosing courtyard*

On the way to the Knesset

The rhythm of the columns echoing the pace of footsteps

Detail of flower structure of judge's patio

View of Jerusalem from panoramic window on judges' level: "Jerusalem in the palm of one's hand" (Ram Karmi)

A turning point: a moment of hestitation before proceeding to the inner gate

To the left: *"Ascent to Jerusalem": Steps leading to the panoramic window*

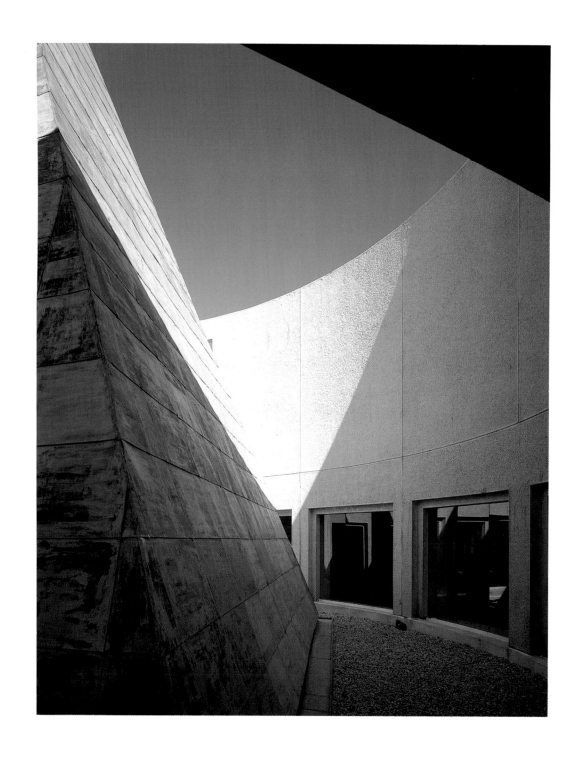

View from judge's level toward copper-clad pyramid and drum wall enveloping it

THE PYRAMID – A GATEHOUSE

*H*aving passed the panoramic window, one enters a pyramid. From outside, only a free-standing form clad in copper is visible; from within, it is a tapered space. Here attention is focused mainly on the light that filters through, and on the converging, geometric floor. The pyramid's singularity derives from its location at the public level, between the entrance and the foyer leading into the courtrooms. No passage to the remainder of the building is visible. The disrupted continuity emphasizes the pyramid's function as an introverted gateway, separating the external world from the Court's domain.

Absalom's Tomb, a Hasmonean burial site in the Kidron Valley below the Temple Mount, was the inspiration for this space. If an opening had been placed at the apex of the Tomb, at certain hours of the day a person standing inside would see a penetrating column of light. Similarly, the four round openings at the top of the pyramid, allow light to be reflected.

The incorporation of elements from an ancient monument in a modern, state edifice is fraught with meaning. The spectrum of analogies is as varied as the needs and messages which converge here. The decision to evoke an element from the Second Temple era may express a desire to transcend time. It lends emphasis to the Jewish people's historic ties to the place, to an earlier form of nationhood.

Yet, the pyramid is not cloaked in an archaic 'guise' – it is not surrounded by the ornate, decorated columns found in Hasmonean tombs. What began as a link to Jerusalem, reinforced by means of a Jewish tomb influenced by Hellenistic culture, is transformed into an abstract, timeless element, devoid of 'national' connotations. Indeed, as one enters the pyramid, the external world and the past are excluded from consciousness. The isolated interior, illuminated from above, suggests transience.

"The law itself has no locality," asserted Lord Stowell, an English judge, in ruling on the relationship between the state's judicial authority and international law. In designing the pyramid, the architects invested much thought and energy in planting it firmly on the ground. This massive and symmetrical geometric object intimates that justice itself would choose to dwell within.

Statutes can be repealed; states can violate or change laws. In the absence of a resolute conviction to uphold laws, they become a mass of meaningless words. The pyramid, in contrast, seems to be stable and immune to change, just as are the eternal principles of the rule of law.

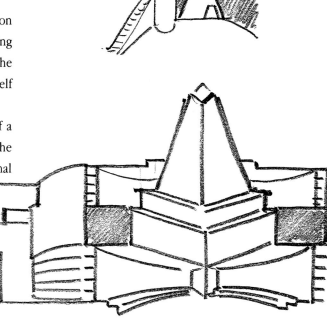

Apex of pyramid: A source of light or internal enlightenment

Pyramid illuminated from within: reflection of green-tinted glass on floor converts the pyramid into a mirror image of itself

THE LIBRARY

The area cirumscribing the pyramid was to be a public space. Only as planning advanced was the library expanded to extend into the public level. This portion of the library is open for general use. The library's second story is intended for sitting justices, while the third is reserved for retired Supreme Court justices.

The library's distinctive feature is an external glass curtain which also serves as an internal partition. The architects sought to emphasize the curvature of the glass partition as a reminder of the passage "he leadeth me in the paths[1] of righteousness" (Psalms 23:3). Here the attempt to realize 'form follows metaphor' is evident. The glass curtain allows one to peer through the panoramic window. It also assumes the role of a transparent partition between the public and the court, a 'window' to the store of legal knowledge. The library has been transformed into a mirror reflecting legal procedures and the rendering of justice within the courtrooms.

In his article "The Court's Power and Limitation,"[2] Justice Moshe Landau wrote: "The Court cannot adjudicate contrary to enacted law, but it can engage in creative interpretation and it can create new rules by way of judge-made law... in areas which are not covered by binding legislation." Looking aside while passing through the pyramid, one senses the "creative interpretation" of the Court, as rendered by the architects. The rulings and precedents found in the legal library bring a vital constant to the building, lending support to new rulings. The architects, on the other hand, have introduced a massive object which becomes a source of reflected light. It is as though the rulings and laws were being tested by a light superior to any possible judgment or juristic interpretation.

1. "Circles" in the Hebrew.
2. **Mishpatim** (Hebrew University Law Journal) 1980: 196, 197.

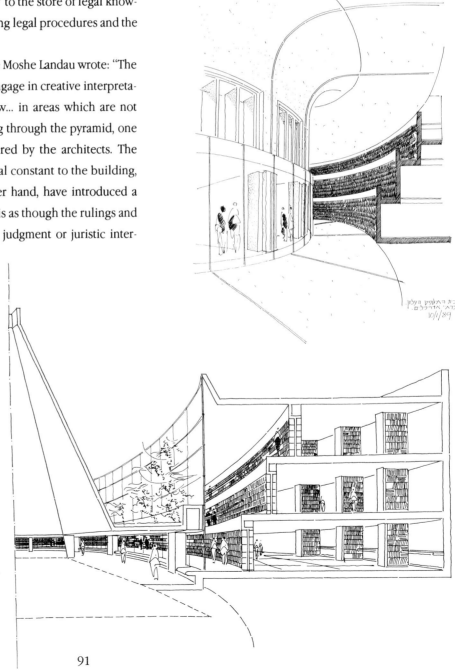

Library interior

THE GRAND FOYER

*T*he pyramid leads to a large space with a low ceiling. This is an in-between zone from which the waiting area of the grand foyer is visible. The threshold, which acts as a crossroad, is more or less equidistant from the two main functions accessible to the public: the registries and the courtrooms. This is the widest part of the foyer. To the south, a window overlooks the Knesset; the window opposite faces the northern entrance to Jerusalem.

The bow-shaped foyer has a dynamic form. Looking west, the field of vision narrows as the distance between the northern wall and the large stone wall decreases. As it contracts to the west, the curved wall creates the illusion that the foyer is even longer than it actually is. The sweep of the massive stone wall deflects the linear succession of courtrooms slightly to the south-west, resulting in a tapered reduction of the public waiting area.

The stone wall highlights the importance of the ceremony taking place within the courtrooms sequestered to the south. After the wall had been clad with stone, Ada Karmi-Melamede spoke of the foyer as a "strong and concise Hebrew sentence" reverberating throughout the structure. Uncertain as to how the wall would evolve, even the architects were pleasantly surprised.

The large foyer allows the Court's power to be projected in full. The height of the stone wall, the thickness of the carved portals and their stepped-up arches, as well as the windows above, all pay homage to Jerusalem: the national sanctum.

Only at first glance does the wall seem 'archaic'. As one draws near it, the seams between the sawn, 15 cm.-thick stones become evident. The narrow interstices are due to the close placement of the stone panels in dry construction, each separately secured to the building's concrete backing with stainless steel hooks. The massive portals do not hold up the stones. The wall is neither supported by them nor does it press against them. Presumably, from the start, the architects had no intention of concealing the gap between the 'archaic wall' and the 'modern means' employed in the foyer. On the contrary, the foyer space proves that modern means are able to project the strength of archaic and traditional stone construction.

The foyer's rich and elaborate architectural effect is also achieved through the use of three-dimensional steel structures. To the north, the white wall opposite the five courtroom portals is composed of a series of cylindrical forms which tend to increase the wall's volume and tighten the space in front. The white volumetric surfaces form inner shells, detached from the concrete backing behind. The circular enclosures function as niches, creating waiting areas for the public. As the cylinders ascend and merge with a hung ceiling, they provide a counterbalance to the weight of the monolithic, horizontal wall.

The great stone wall

The vertical, white enclaves are unadorned. Each niche is arranged in a semi-circle facing the large public area. The niches allow visitors a measure of necessary privacy, to think and reflect at a point as far removed from the courtrooms as possible. The prevailing atmosphere of respect for the individual may be attributed to the niches' narrow shape and the light reflecting from above.

The dynamic equilibrium between the stone wall and the row of niches opposite – between a hard, massive material and the seemingly weightless, ascending forms – contributes to the complex composition of the public level. The public moves within a space which provokes a confrontation between the 'modern' white components and the 'traditional' archaic wall. In the architects' explanation:

> "Until we put up this building, we believed that architecture must always search for a common denominator which projects its presence upon the building's components and is nurtured by them in turn. The work on the Supreme Court Building introduced us to a greater complexity. The foyer organizes the various parts and mediates between them while maintaining its own personality, independent of all the other spaces emanating from it. The foyer does not obscure the differences between the courthouse's various units but, rather, intensifies them."

Perspective of Grand Foyer: the archaic wall and its five thick portals constitute the public facade of the building. The entry into the courtrooms is a transition from a modern, flowing space to a more 'classical', vertical one.

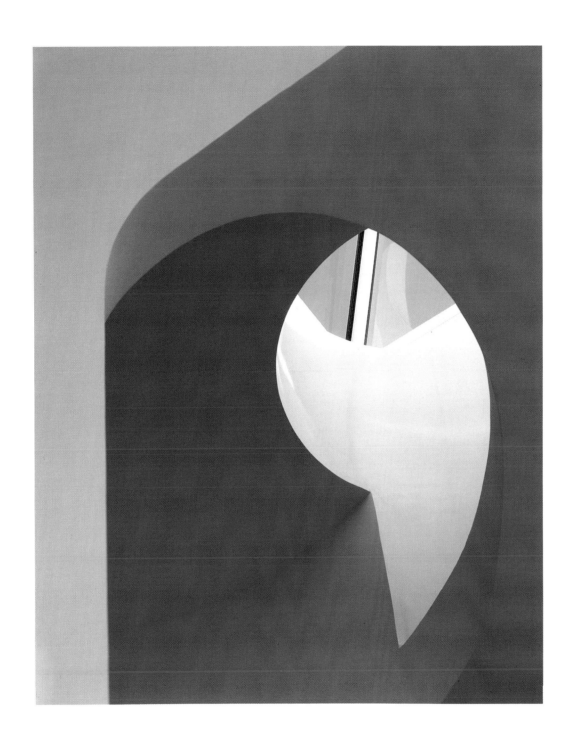

One of a series of openings for light in Grand Foyer

THE STONE WALL

*T*he foyer's stone wall is the building's 'spine' and orders its division. As planning advanced, it became evident that the foyer was a fragment of the greater urban order outside the courthouse. Just as the panoramic window addresses the centre of the City and East Jerusalem, so the wall refers to the space north of the building. It is a segment of a circle extending far beyond the Supreme Court, radiating from the Convention Centre and the entrance to the City.

The wall seems to rise from a place far deeper than the base of the building, from the bowels of the earth. It is a natural constant to which the building must submit. At the panoramic window, it breaks free of the facade. If externally the building is reminiscent of the Mandatory Period, the foyer's stone wall is a far more ancient element. It seems able to bear any load and to overcome the resistance of the building's modern walls. This is not a wall that suggests: "I love the building, I will not go out free." To the contrary, it wills the structure and the perimeter walls to say: "I love my master" (Exodus 21:5). Throughout the building the architects have emphasized the wall's absolute independence, by maintaining a constant distance between it and the adjoining elements.

In their statement of intent, Karmi-Melamede and Karmi expressed a natural and passionate love for the land and its landscapes. This love found expression in the use of local, unhewn stone, light brown to reddish-brown in color. "These are the pastel colors of compassion, unlike those of basalt and granite," said Karmi-Melamede. The term coined by the architects and building coordinator Eliezer Rahat for the stone used in the stone wall was "heel-stone" or "crust-stone." This alludes to the end crusts, like in bread, remaining after a 'loaf' of stone has been sawn, pieces which are usually discarded. The architects first noticed these offcuts in a waste heap during a visit to a local quarry.

Chiseling is a form of styling, and style always implies a memory of things long past. Raw material, on the other hand, is ageless. This is what led the architects to reverse the usual procedures. Here the sawn off 'cultured' side of the stone is hooked to the wall's concrete spine, while the natural, unworked side is left visible. Although civilization and the twentieth century have left their mark on the stone, this is not what strikes the eye. The rough stone is strong and convincing, yet leaves room for reflection.

When work on the wall first began, Karmi explained why he had selected such massive stones. He pointed to several young men who had just completed their military service and had chosen to work in construction. Calling them "Nimrods," he said: "A wall like this needs many Nimrods," workers who will keep pace, for whom nothing will stand in the way of construction. The choice of Nimrod was no coincidence. In an attempt to represent the original, authentic links with Cana'an, the ancient Land of Israel, Karmi drew upon the well-known sculpture of the mythical Biblical figure by Izhak Danziger. Karmi linked two Biblical books from different periods. He replicated and

The entrance to the courtrooms is composed of three flat arches carved into the great stone wall, accentuating the transition from an ancient, unhewn element to the courtrooms' static and symmetrical spaces. The rectangles of brilliant light on the courtroom doors are reflections of the exterior, projected from openings in the wall opposite. Above each portal is a deep-set window facing an internal corridor through which the judges enter the courtrooms.

Above: *North wall of Grand Foyer and public waiting area* Right: *steps leading to cafeteria*

replaced Nimrod with King Solomon's "threescore and ten thousand that bare burdens," the builders of the First Temple. In an article published in *Perspecta* (26, 1990), Karmi-Melamede describes the relationship between the stone wall and the Old City walls in the following words: "Jerusalem is an urban island contained by a wall that seems to grow from the earth as an organic extension of the hilly terrain." The layers of stone carved from the earth's crust have become a horizontal bas relief, inserted in the soil and representing its inherent characteristics, rather than any archaeological aspect. The importance of the stone wall lies in the sharp contrast it creates between the static, historical spaces to its south (where the judges' chambers, registries and courtrooms are located), and the modern, asymmetrical space to its north: "As one proceeds south, the portals of the 'past,' lead to a static and more familiar place. As one walks north, one comes upon a world of modern architecture, a flowing, unending space."

"It is a well known axiom that the law of a people must be studied in the light of its total national life," said Justice Shimon Agranat in a landmark Supreme Court decision.[1] He referred to Israel's Declaration of Independence as a vital mirror of "the law of the people," without according it the status of constitutional law. In the absence of a formal constitution, broad interpretation of the Declaration of Independence is likely to ensure that the country's laws remain faithful to the Basic Laws, to individual and minority rights including freedom of speech and conscience. Although the stone wall could not be made to signify the wide and symbolic meaning accruing to the concept 'the law of a people,' the architects tried to convey the widest possible interpretation of national life.

The raw stone gives one the feeling of being only an insignificant part of a larger cycle. Standing in the foyer beside these stones, one is forced to abandon part of one's self. The words of the writer J.M. Berdyczewski come to mind. Writing at the end of the nineteenth century, he cited the desire "to be Hebrews, instantaneously and in one breath, nurtured by a single source."[2] The return to the ancient land has always been at the heart of Zionism. In Karmi's view, the raw stone wall carved out of the land may represent the idea of 'a single source,' stressing the Zionist revival.

The wall may be seen as the architectural realization of the desire "to be Hebrews instantaneously and in one breath." At the same time, a certain idealization of archaic experience implied in the term "Nimrods," is compelling because it makes us all equal: Jews, Christians, Muslims, Circassians, Druse. All are led to feel equally distant from the wall. It is as if the local material legitimizes the differences. This concept reflects the juridic principle according to which the political, ethnic and religious associations of all of Israel's citizens are safeguarded. The ancient character of the stone reads democracy.

Above all, the large wall is an event in itself. Monumentality is generally perceived through the dimensions of size and height. Here, the dimension of time is also evident. It is difficult to walk rapidly past these stones. One is forced to slow down, or so it seems. Even if one's pace increases, one cannot ignore the need to join the flow of movement dictated by the wall, as it envelops all comers in an experience greater than oneself.

1. Kol Ha'am Co., Ltd. vs the Minister of the Interior, the High Court of Justice 53/73 P.D. (7), p 871.
2. J.M. Berdyczewski "At the crossroads/ an open letter to Ahad Ha'am," **Hashiloah** 1896/1897, Vol I: 154-159.

HIERARCHY AND LIGHT

*C*eremonial rites seek to reinforce distance and hierarchy, and to confer stability on social rules and order. Some of these rites are so ancient that they are accepted without question, although their rationale may not be evident. The authority invested in the Supreme Court, as the architectural programme noted, is self-evident and does not require pomp or undue emphasis.

At the same time, the sense of hierarchy within the Supreme Court Building is not simply a function of the prescribed protocol of the judicial process. It is expressed in the balance between the wall's height and massiveness, and the feeling of shelter it instills. The wall's solidity weighs in favour of the Supreme Court's absolute authority over the individual. The wall 'observes' the public from all angles, but the individual sees only a section. It is the inability to step back and increase one's visual field that makes the wall so compelling.

The hierarchy is further emphasized by the strict distance maintained between judges and public. Beyond the windows overlooking the five entrances, is a corridor leading from the judges' chambers to the courtrooms. The design of the windows accentuates the depth of the wall and the massiveness of its stones. All along the public level there are 'intermediate zones' in which one may rest, unburdened by the prevailing sense of hierarchy. The dynamic structure of the public level allows a constant flow. The public access to the Administration courtyard, the panoramic window, the windows with views of the southern and northern parts of the building, the steps leading from the foyer to the garden beyond the courtrooms – all these offer options for repose.

The ceremony and hierarchy called for in the competition brief have been successfully realized. The Supreme Court and the client took into consideration the time visitors would spend in the building. Even if not everyone has a free moment, even if not all are interested in 'studying' the building's architecture, a visitor cannot help but be aware of the solemnity of the occasion.

However, the building envisaged by the architects has been invaded by a random, unpredictable and ephemeral force: light. In contrast to the heavy foyer wall, the light is buoyant and dynamic. It sets a festive mood and provides subtle shadings as the day wears on and as the seasons change. The light is a constant reminder of the world outside, hinting that the events taking place within this space, solemn as they may be, are part of a greater and more comprehensive reality.

THE COURTROOMS

*E*ntering the courtrooms one proceeds from the primordial stone wall to a static, symmetrical space, a passage from the symbols of natural and historic justice to the state's tangible laws. Hewn into the foyer wall to the north and shielded by the judges' consultation rooms to the south, the courtrooms are the most secluded area on the public level.

In direct contrast to the building entrance – where the public ascends to an illuminated space, the foyer with its panoramic window – upon entering the courtrooms the process is reversed. Once inside, a pleasant dimness prevails. It is as though the courtrooms were tucked away, deep in the rocky terrain. The sheltered spaces reflect the spirit of the law, as perceived by the architects. Like the law itself, the courtrooms are deeply rooted in something vast and timeless: the land.[1]

The judges proceed directly from their chambers through two doors to the judges' bench (alcove), without contact with the public or with prisoners whose appeals are being heard. The public enters from the foyer. Prisoners are taken by elevator from two levels below and brought in through a side door. They sit in the dock, to the right of the alcove, between the public and the judges. (See courtroom no. 4, p. 111).

The design concept of the courtrooms is identical to that of the foyer: 'a room within a room.' Cast concrete walls and celings form the backing for suspended volumetric structures. Actually, each courtroom is an inner shell with floating vaults. In two courtrooms, the columns appear to be bearing the weight of the vaults. Behind them, dry-hung Mitzpe Ramon stone covers the concrete walls. Each courtroom is based on the geometric concept of two equal squares, with judges and advocates seated in the one to the south and the public located in the northern square.

The courtrooms were designed to reflect the principle that the process of rendering justice is open to every individual and each person has a right to legal redress. This principle finds expression when citizens appeal directly to the High Court of Justice to address a perceived governmental infringement of their basic rights. The openness takes form in the basilica layout of the courtrooms, the style the architects found most appropriate for this purpose.

Everyone involved in the planning process wanted the courtrooms to be isolated from the outside world so that those within could concentrate on the events taking place. Although the judges are seated on a raised platform in a classical alcove, public access to the courtrooms is not by means of a centre aisle, as in most houses of worship, but along aisles on each side of the courtroom. The judges too do not enter from the centre, but from the side of the alcove. Public movement in the middle of the hall (at the nave) has been eliminated, so as not to distract from the legal discourse: "In these courtrooms it is neither the judges nor the public, but the law that plays the leading role," said one of the

Courtroom No. 1 This is a small hall of 135 sq.m., seating 40. The base of its vaults is emphasized by a stepped cornice, above which a series of narrow, perpendicular slits introduce light. The public section is roofed by a barrel-vault which becomes a dome over the judges' alcove. There is no arcade. The white, plastered walls descend to the floor, forming a continuous envelope.

judges. The two semi-circular tables for the judges and for the advocates demarcate the circle of dialogue and stress the centrality of the legal discourse.

That discourse is usually limited to judges and advocates. Nevertheless, the public attending the hearings is made to feel that a certain deference is called for. The symmetrical order of the space, the different elevations and the frontal seating arrangement for the public project the Court's authority. If in the round space of the library the public senses that the law is accessible, in the courtrooms a tangible distance is felt.

The elevated platform undoubtedly underlines this relationship – and not by chance. The Court's legal precedents constitute, as we know, a part of Israel's Positive Law. In the Court's rulings, civil and individual rights are deliberated upon and given definition. The public is witness to a process culminating in binding decisions on fundamental matters. Yet the formal distance between the judges and the public is tempered by the architects' obvious propensity for traditional design, which instils a measure of familiarity.

The courtroom atmosphere commands awe, but not fear. This results from the geometry employed, the extensive use of wood and the indirect natural light that pervades the space. The light is soft, not dazzling. In the Russian Compound, the Supreme Court's previous location, sound – or rather noise – was in constant attendance. The thick walls of the old building could not block out the relentless din. In the new courtrooms, light serves as a link to the world outside; the becoming stillness is heard.

Along the aisles the patterns of circulation and structure (columns and arches) are orchestrated by the light. The indirect illumination of the aisles and the direct sunlight striking the apse reflect the need for both openness and ceremony. One is reminded of Louis Kahn's statement: "Structure is the giver of light."[2] This is no less true in the courtrooms than in the foyer. The lighting is largely indirect: the rays of sun coming from the south hit a deep light-funnel and ricochet, shedding light on the inner circle of dialogue.

1. See, Statement of Intent.
2. **Light is the Theme: Louis I. Kahn & the Kimbell Art Foundation Comments on Architecture by Louis Kahn,** compiled by Nell E. Johnson. Kimbell Art Foundation, Fort Worth Texas, 1975.

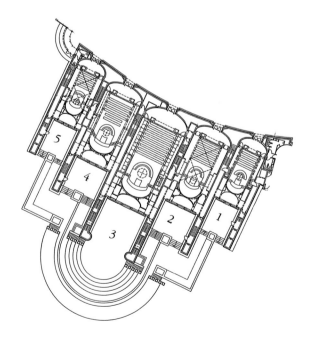

Courtroom No. 2 *This is a medium-sized, cross-vaulted hall of 220 sq.m., seating 70, with two arches along each aisle. The arches are supported by two adjacent columns at the centre of the room. Light mainly penetrates through the partly covered aisles on either side of the courtroom. Circular openings are set in the eastern and western walls. The vaults are made of glass reinforced concrete (G.R.C.).*

Courtroom No. 3 *This courtroom, seating 150, is the largest (280 sq.m.) and most representative. Nine square, steel columns faced with wood panels define the partly covered aisles through which the public enters. A half-domed ceiling connects the judges' alcove with the barrel-vault over the public section. Two rows of long, narrow slits at the base of the vault allow indirect light to penetrate.*

Courtroom No. 4 *This is a medium-sized courtroom of 220 sq.m., seating 70. On either side of the hall there are four square columns faced with wood panels. The dome of the alcove merges with the courtroom's barrel-vaulted ceiling.*

Courtroom No. 5 *This small, cross-vaulted hall has an overall area of 135 sq.m. and seats 40. Along each aisle there are two G.R.C. arches 'supported' by columns. The junction between the arches is concealed by light fixtures.*

THE COURTYARD: ADMINISTRATION LEVEL

*A*left turn from the foyer leads to the judges' wing and the Administration below, two storeys disposed around the perimeter of a closed courtyard. The first story houses the Administration and the Court Registries; the upper story – the judges' chambers, which are generally barred to the public. In contrast to the massive presence of raw stone in the foyer, particularly prominent here is the finely hewn and detailed white stone. An arcade with heavy plastered arches surrounds the courtyard.

Advocates and the public tend to routine business matters at the northern part of the courtyard where the various registries are located: Civil Division, Criminal Division, High Court of Justice Division. Surrounding the courtyard is the Administration: secretariat, registrar's chambers, deputy registrar's chambers, chief clerk, probation officer, semi-active files and other secretarial offices.

The human scale of the Administration level lends an intimate character to the public's contact with the Court. Although the prevailing hierarchy has not escaped the design of the courtyard, it is only adroitly hinted at. Beyond the high window in the southern apse, a corridor leads to the President's chambers. On the northern side of the courtyard, above the Administration level, a large balcony looks out from the judges' lounge, where the judges meet and receive visitors and official guests.

An arcade links the Administration offices to the north with the courtyard. The design of the courtyard and arcade flooring unify the courtyard and the interior of this wing. Upon entering, one suddenly finds oneself in 'a different building.' Passing from the foyer's flowing space, one encounters the traditional image of a monastic courtyard, a Madrasa (Islamic academy), a palace-like atmosphere. The element of water has been incorporated into the courtyard, echoing the wells and cisterns of Jerusalem's Islamic and Christian buildings. In the southern apse, there is a small pool into which a narrow copper channel spills its water.

In arid, desert climates, water assumes a sacred dimension – it is a mirror of the heavens. The introduction of water intimates the local atmosphere and climate. Although its presence does not directly influence the building's image, it confers a dimension of sanctity evoking the concept: "Righteousness shall look down[1] from heaven."

The southern apse and the lay-out of the entire courtyard, the balcony on the north and the covered arcades on either side, led Gabriel Peretz, the general contractor, to misgivings. His apprehensions were dispelled when he learned that this classical form is not foreign to synagogues from the Byzantine period. In the Second Temple (early Roman) era, synagogues served as places of assembly, not as regular venues for reciting prayers and reading the Bible. Those functions were confined to the Temple.[2] A characteristic element in some of the late Roman and Byzantine synagogues is a raised stone slab (bema) which served as the focus of liturgical rites. Archaeological excavations show that there was a Torah shrine opposite the bema, and sometimes in the wall oriented towards Jerusalem. This is how the finds from synagogues in the 'Jewish' Galilee have been interpreted.[3] According to findings from the ancient synagogues at Beit Alfa and Hamat Gader, it was only after the destruction of the Second Temple that an apse was combined with the more ancient bema.

In a 1988 letter to the architects, Engineer Dan Wind expressed concern about possible Islamic connotations. But neither Islamic associations nor the resemblance to a church apse, such as is found in basilicas, alter the fact that above all the apse in the courtyard of arches recalls the Roman Triumphal Arch. This element was incorporated into the courtyard. Instead of the arch being faced with ceramic tile (the architects' original intention), it was plastered and whitewashed and is elegantly simple. The architects made no effort to disguise the origin of the arched courtyard. It is a likeness of that found in the Rockefeller Museum. The idea of adapting the museum courtyard was part of the architects' overall concept, which sought to capture the essence of Jerusalem through architectural archetypes.

The courtyard, static and totally detached from the outside world, keenly suggests the heavens' presence. In the summer, the sun beats down on the blazing stone floor which reflects the brilliant light. Three arches are set one within the other, their thickness pleasing to the eye. The level of the courtyard is higher than that of the arcaded passage. The shaded stone openings beneath the arches serve as 'built-in' benches, a refuge from the harshly lit public exterior. "In modern construction, the dividing line between the exterior and the interior is a wall about twenty centimeters thick," says Karmi-Melamede. "Here, in the courtyard, it is far greater. This was deliberate: the partition between the arcaded ambulatory and the open, unshielded public section works to the benefit of the visitors seated in the shade of the arches. The thickness of the wall creates an in-between space, allowing passage between the two zones."

The glass windows arranged in rows on either side of the courtyard, reflect one another as they elongate the perspective. Administration rooms whose windows open onto the courtyard were taken into account: the level of the rooms is higher than that of the arcaded pedestrian passage, allowing those seated inside to look out, without having their field of vision blocked by passers-by. Pedestrians moving along the arcade do not see those working in the rooms.

1. "Is reflected," in the original Hebrew, Psalms 85:12.
2. "Second Temple Period Synagogue," in: L.I. Levine (ed.), **Ancient Synagogues Revealed**, Jerusalem 1981, 19-VII.
3. "Synagogues of the Galilee," **ibid.**, 42-51.

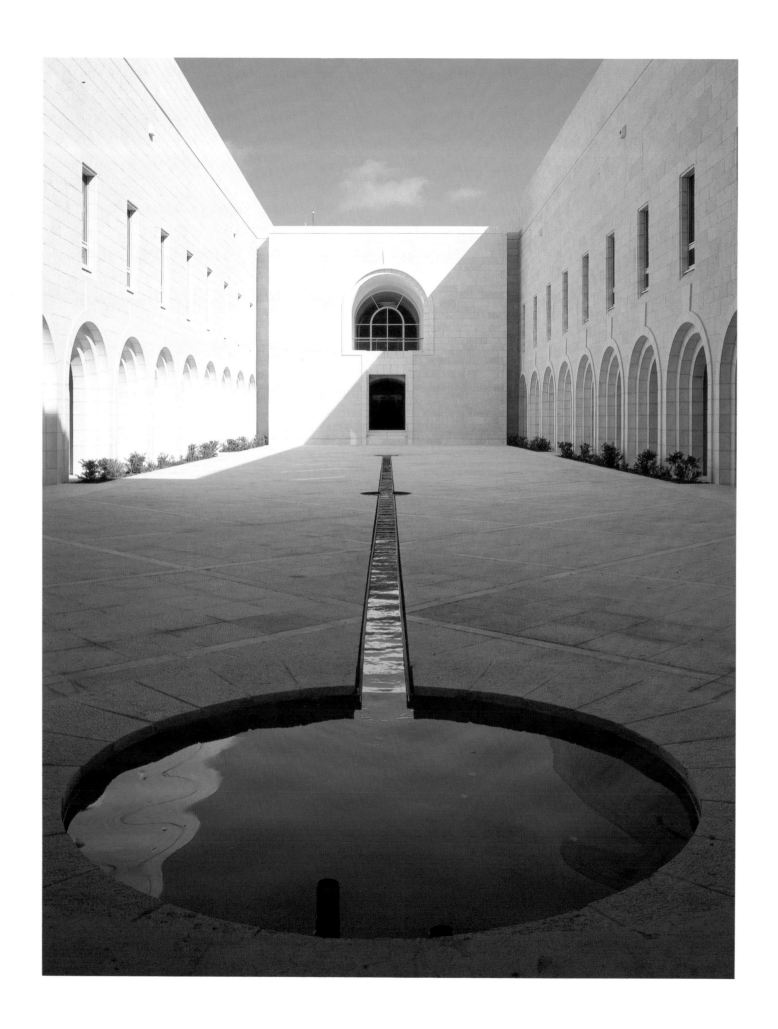

Above: *Courtyard's white stone flooring delineated by glass inlays*
Left: *View of Judges' Courtyard facing north. A channel of water bisects the length of the courtyard and reflects the sky.*

View of Judges' Courtyard through covered arcade

Peripheral corridor of Administration wing

View of Judges' Courtyard from public waiting area at Administration level

THE COURTYARD FROM THE JUDGES' LEVEL

*T*he judges' chambers are located just above the Administration. The functional division between the two levels allows the judges to contemplate and deliberate without distraction. They have separate access, hidden from the public eye, to the library and the courtrooms. From the courtyard, there are no signs of connection between the two levels. From above, the arched courtyard seems like the judges' private domain.

The fact that the President of the Court's chambers are located at the southern end of the judges' wing helped determine the courtyard's final form. According to the original scheme, the President's chambers were separate from the others and located on the uppermost level of the library, at the northern end of the building. This was changed at the request of the President, who felt that the proposed lay-out would cause unnecessary division and distance. The pattern of peripheral movement at the judges' level is now continuous, as in the Registry below.

At the eastern side of the judges' level there are seven chambers; the western facade has six. Each chamber is a separate suite, including articled clerks' room and secretary's office. The judge's room contains a work area surrounded by a personal library, a lounge area and a small patio. The chambers walls are made of gypsum panels; the ceilings are suspended plastered vaults. Light enters the judge's and clerks rooms through large, common windows opening onto the patio.

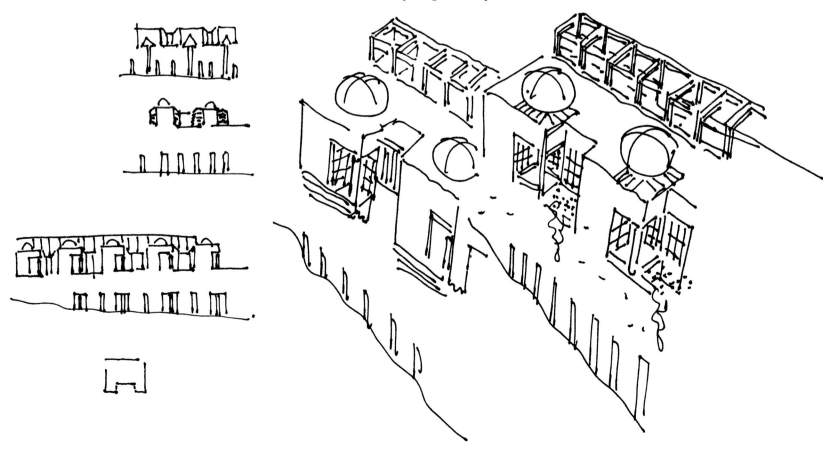

Right: *Conference room adjacent to President's chambers*

Above: *Large Conference room to the north of the judges' wing*
Below: *Cross-vaulted alcove of judges' lounge*

President's chambers

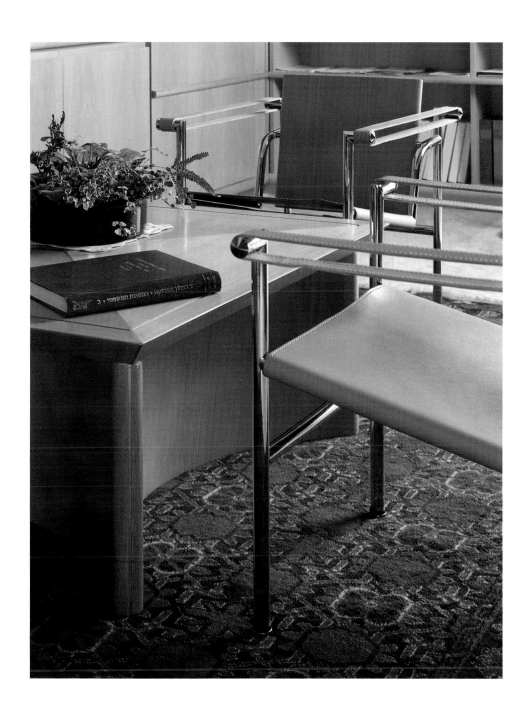

Detail of seating area in President's chambers

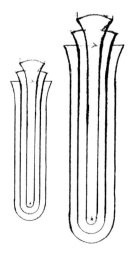

Typical entrance to judge's chamber with wooden door-frame reminiscent of court-room entry. Silver mezuzah was the final design by silversmith David Gumbel of blessed memory; signage by Peter Szmuk

BUILDING AND CONSTRUCTION DETAILS

(The architects' perspective)

"*T*he building addresses various strata of local culture, ancient and modern. It is seemingly composed of four autonomous parts, separated by two axes of super-imposed and intersecting movement. Actually, the transition from one section to another involves a grand and dynamic circular pattern, starting at the entrance level and proceeding towards the courtroom level above. This movement is directional and entails a gradual sequence, a stepping back in time.

"The circular, self-generated movement is dictated by the building itself, although not confined to it. It is perceived as a fragment of a larger urban circulation pattern in which space mediates between the language of today and of the past. The simple order of the different parts is experienced as a set of intricate layers. Thus, the procession within the building becomes part of a greater process.

"The building facades are not uniform. They carefully preserve the memories of historic Jerusalem, of a miniature city enclosed by a wall. And yet, they hint at the new and different events taking place within. The facades accommodate themselves to the sloping, natural terrain, adjusting their height accordingly. The fronts zealously guard a constant, unequivocal skyline which circumscribes the building and creates a new datum: the roof, an archaeological garden of modern architectural forms.

"The building's layering is both horizontal and vertical. The horizontal penetration into the core (courtrooms, arches, courtyard) is a glimpse into the past; the vertical penetration to the roof is a peek into contemporary times. Layering, is expressed by the relationship between mass and contained void. Here it is in constant flux, expressing the architectural interplay at each level.

"In the past, massive, mainly stone construction was the norm; a building's perimeter wall was simultaneously its structural support and climatic shield. Walls were thick and openings deep, as though carved from the natural stone itself. The transition from room to room was achieved through the depth of the wall and assumed an architecture of its own. These 'in-between zones' punctuated the architectural sequence in time and space (see "The Stone Wall").

"With the introduction of lighter building materials, it became possible to compress the internal and external shells into one thin monolithic mass, whose properties were similar to those of the thick stone wall. Once the structural element was reduced, one could disengage the building envelope from its support elements (beams and columns), and the ceiling from the floor above it.

"Likewise, one can now decrease mass and its presence, thereby expanding the effective space and releasing the walls from their load-bearing function. In modern architecture, a thin technological membrane suffices (see page 154).

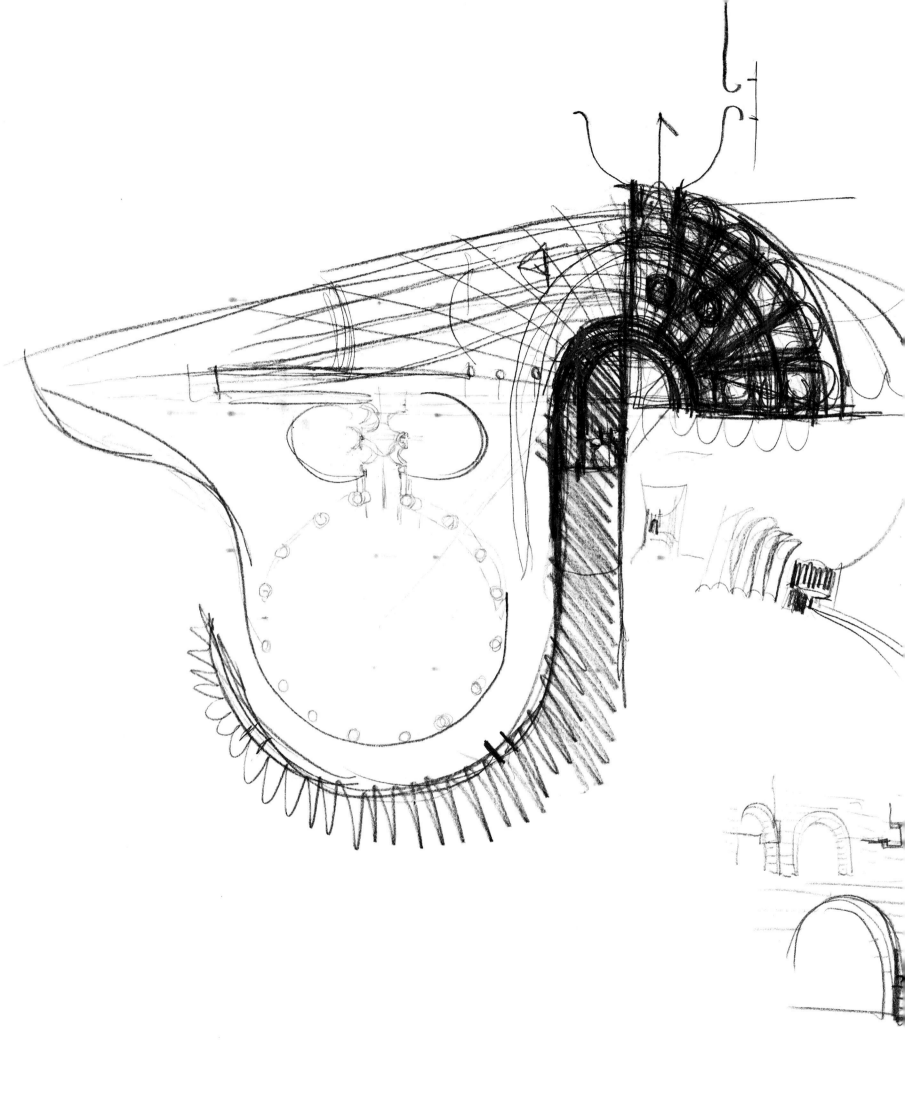

"We utilized all these means. We created a sensation of depth through simulated traditional construction, the play of alternating light and shade, and the sense of weight and security projected by ancient stone walls. Depth was also achieved by detailing, and even more so by the introduction of contained space for both visual and utilitarian purposes. We exchanged mass for void for 'in-between space,' separating the stone wall from the plastered one (see page 147).

"We 'restored' the aesthetic of the massive stone wall by wet construction of concrete backing and stone cladding. Corner-stones were used to conceal the actual thickness of the cladding. The facades once again have a traditional, vertical character and the appearance of a load-bearing wall. We opened up long, narrow slots in these walls, with typical lintels and keystones. We also created plastered arcades framed by sets of converging arches (see pages 145-148).

"Throughout, we perceived the stone walls as constant elements of Jerusalem. This called for rigid construction details. As in older buildings, the architectural language of the facades expresses load transfer, hinting at the continuity inscribed into the horizontal levels. Only the inner plaster shell is flexible and variable. Just as it draws closer to the curved surfaces and ceilings, confronting memories beyond the city walls, so too it contends with thin, volumetric membranes and the idiom of contemporary architecture (see page 155). The free plaster shell ascends, as though seeking to escape; the stone wall presses down, as if to rejoin the earth. Throughout, we perceived these contradictions as complementary. Only in the foyer area did we intensify the tension: the walls swing outward, confronting one another, drawing closer without ever touching (see page 153).

"The volumetric plastered skin, in wet or dry construction, recedes from the external wall. In distancing itself from the concrete backing of ceilings and walls, the plaster both reflects and manipulates the light.

"The space between the plaster skin and the stone wall is a formed volume, terminating in a 'light cell', like a reflecting light-funnel of white surfaces (see pages 158 and 160). The funnel transforms the raw light into human light, allowing it to be reflected in a palate of shades and shapes against the wall and the floor opposite. The light cell tames the natural, blinding light, rendering it pure and soft.

"Throughout the building, layering is exploited to modify light. The more sculpted the light cells, the more efficiently do they mediate between natural, bright light and the desired, muted effect. Light cells are dispersed throughout the building: linearly along the foyer's stone wall and in a scattered pattern on the white wall. Together, they create a new, three-dimensional fabric whose presence is evident everywhere. The unique properties of this weave result from the reflected natural light. It is employed in the 'connective tissue' of the building for movement, rest and 'idling.' The fabric does not exist to serve or to enhance other events but is an event in and of itself, imbuing all others with significance. Light has been exploited as a building material, perhaps the most important of them all."

East Elevation

The east elevation, like all the others, is not homogeneous. Long narrow slits are carved into the stone wall (library, to the right). They are reminiscent of typical openings in traditional stone construction. The square openings to the left reveal the volumetric nature of the stone wall and its inner plastered layer. The large window protruding from the envelope and 'leaning' against the great stone wall, is a place of its own.

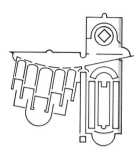

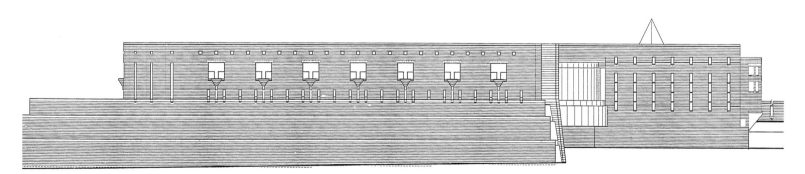

Window in Judge's Chambers

The internal, plastered wall curves away from the plane of the stone, combining the chambers' various functions by creating a uniform front of plaster and glass. The separation between the two layers generates a personal, introverted scale within the large public dimension which overlooks the city. The contained volume between plaster and stone diffuses the light.

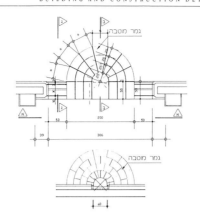

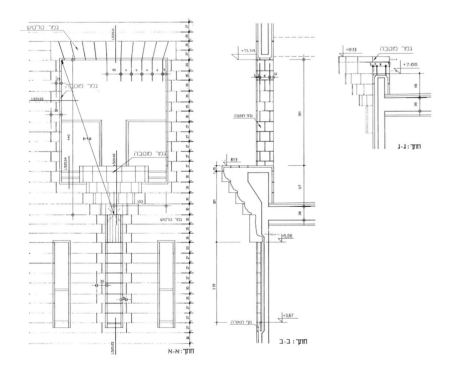

Library Window

The window is carved into the massive stone wall, which is composed of a concrete backing and a thin stone cladding. The wall is treated as a homogeneous mass, with corner-stones concealing the actual thickness of the cladding.

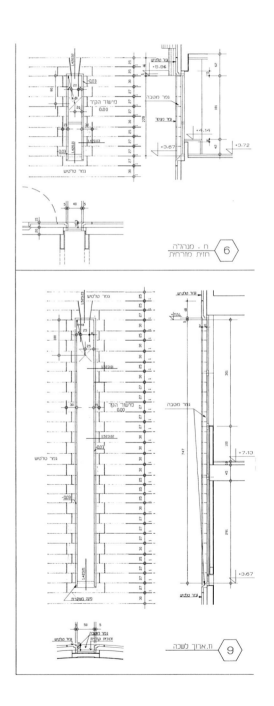

Window Facing East

The large window facing east issues from the joint between the sinuous glass wall that wraps around the library and the great stone wall which bisects the building. Here, the internal space juts out, accentuating the independence of the great stone wall and its urban scale. The window is a place in its own right.

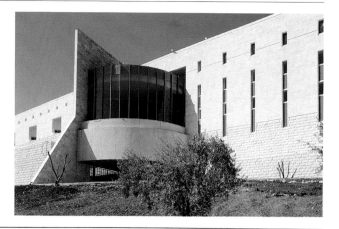

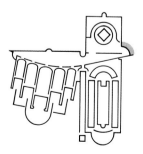

135

North Elevation

This is a facade of load-bearing walls made of
massive stone from which the library and cafeteria stairways protrude. The entrance appears to
be hewn into the stone wall at the intersection
of the north-south and the east-west axes.

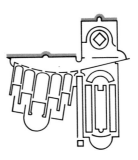

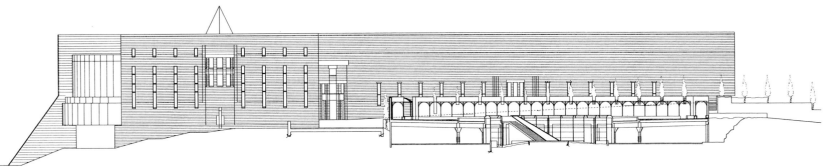

Library Stairway

The stairway is accentuated throughout its
height by vertical reveals and by the structural
support at its base. This stair links the storeys of
the library; its lower part is an emergency exit.

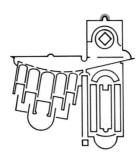

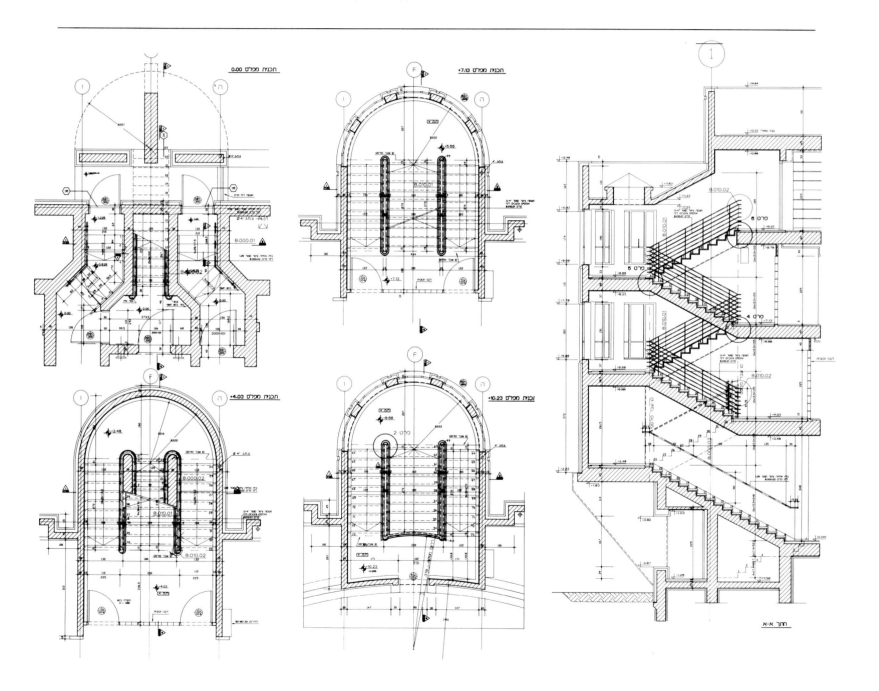

137

Entrance

The doorway is seemingly carved into the wall; the northern and western walls are perpendicular to one another and continue far beyond their point of intersection. An introverted, in-between space is thus created, sheltered and lit from above. Within the doorway, a set of smaller gates is visible: the outer frame of the gateway addresses the city scale, the smaller opening – the building scale.

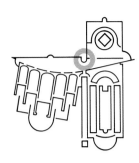

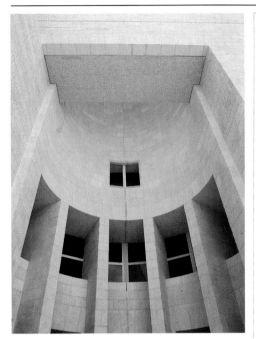

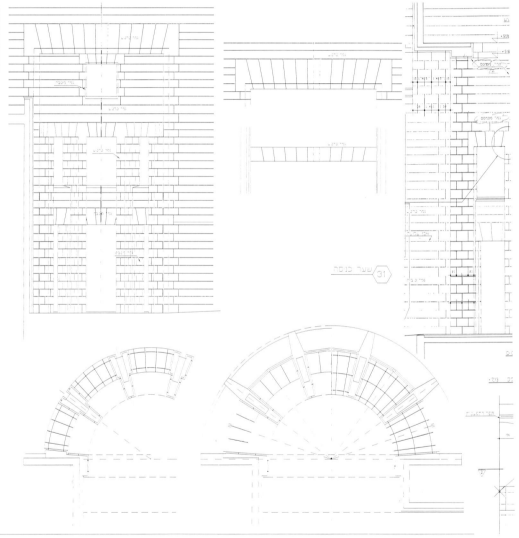

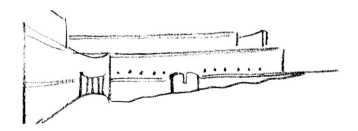

Cafeteria Stairway

The stairway rises from the ground and is accentuated by a vertical reveal. The stairway's stone walls are treated as load-bearing walls: the stone and the concrete backing act as a cohesive whole, concealing the aluminum frames. The openings read frameless.

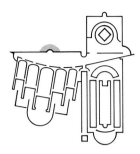

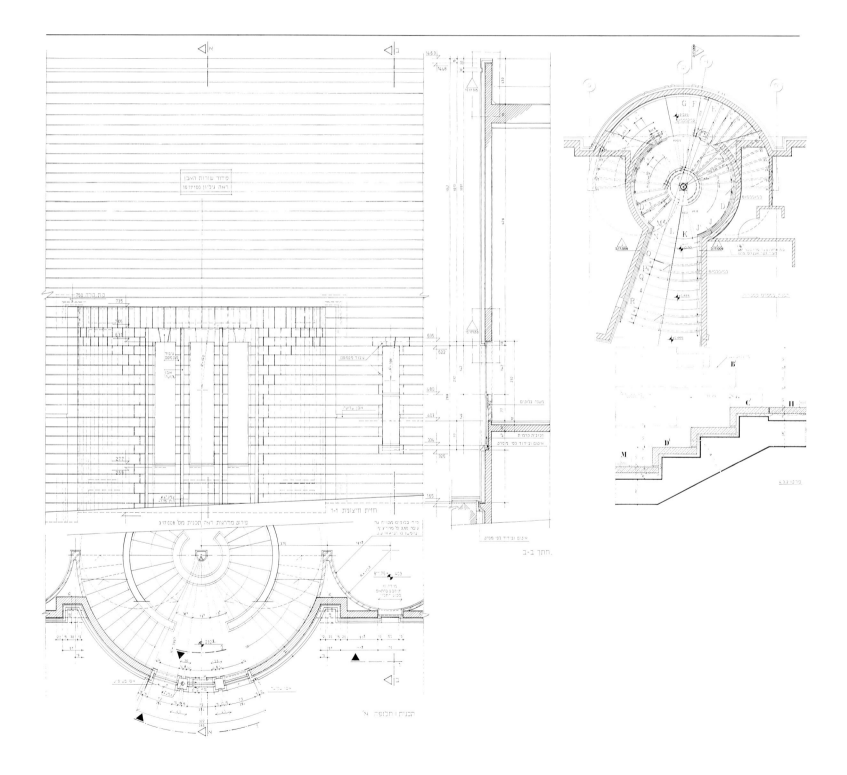

The cafeteria stairway is detailed as an integral
part of the supporting stone wall. It is made up
of massive stone blocks and devoid of seams.

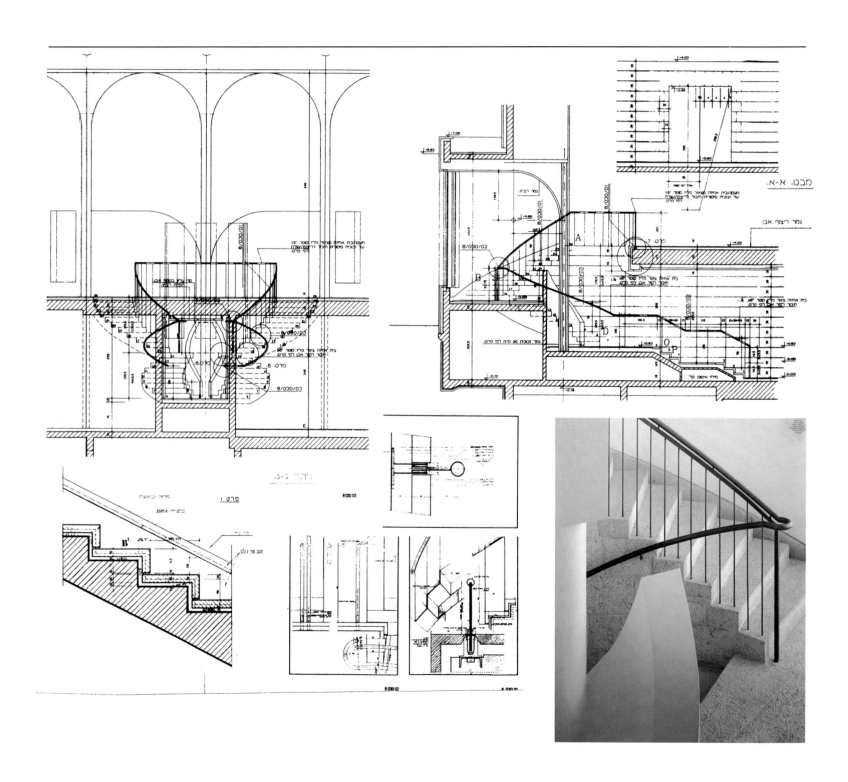

140

West Elevation

The intersection of the axes bisecting the building is evident. The stone perimeter-walls act as load-bearing walls, allowing the main foyer to break through and terminate in a glass and steel structure.

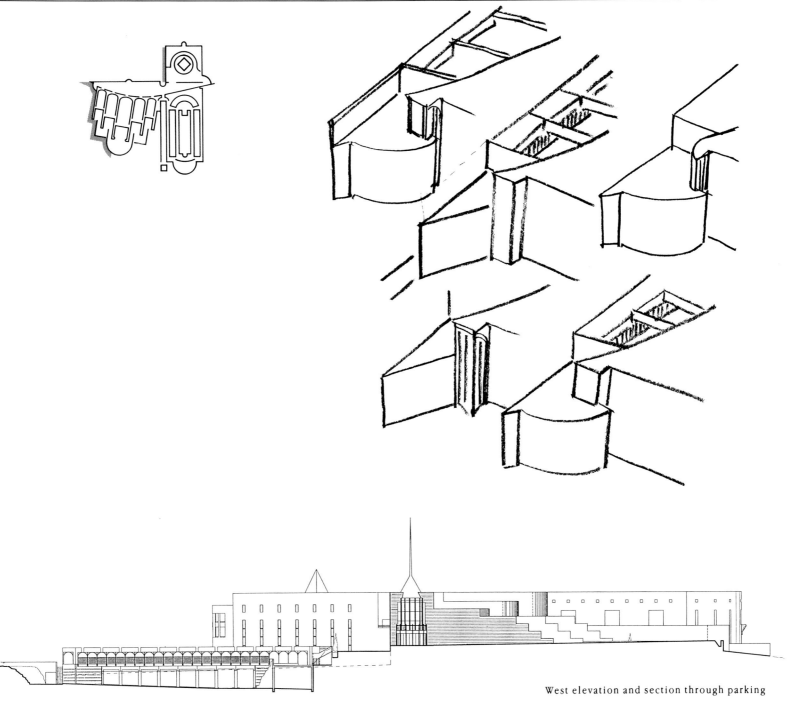

West elevation and section through parking

South Elevation

This facade is bisected by the north-south axis – the gateway leading to the Knesset. Here, more than elsewhere, the building breaks up into its individual parts. These express the individual scale of the courtrooms, the judges' chambers and the judges' cascading corridors.

The courtrooms are nestled into the hillside, their fronts gradually descending to the 'amphitheater' facing the cafeteria. Each courtroom is free-standing within its own domain and delineated by inclined walls which link the building's roof with the courtroom gardens.

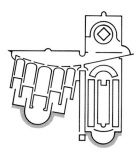

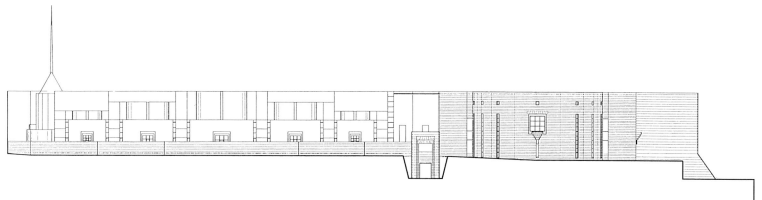

Section through courtrooms and Knesset route

142

Details of Courtroom Gardens

Each courtroom, detached from the surrounding walls, is accentuated by vertical slots. The circular forms of the courtroom stages project above the skyline of each courtroom and recede from the south elevation, expressing the independence of the different layers. The stages are dressed in bush-hammered concrete, the vertical and horizontal seams emphasizing the casting.

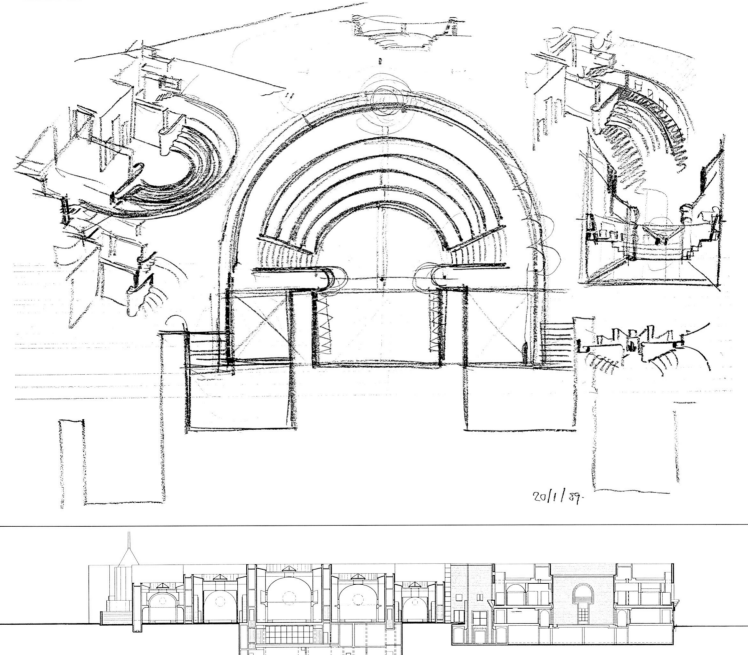

East-West section through courtrooms and Administration wing

Window of President's chambers pays homage to Eric Mendelsohn

The Knesset Axis

The Knesset axis is bordered by high stone walls with flat arches, delineating a shaded and plastered inner arcade. Deep, wide columns lined with massive corner-stones form an integral part of the stone wall above. The width of the columns shields the arcades extending behind. The arcades are elongated rooms stemming from the main entrance while shying away from it.

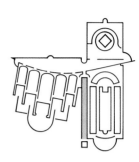

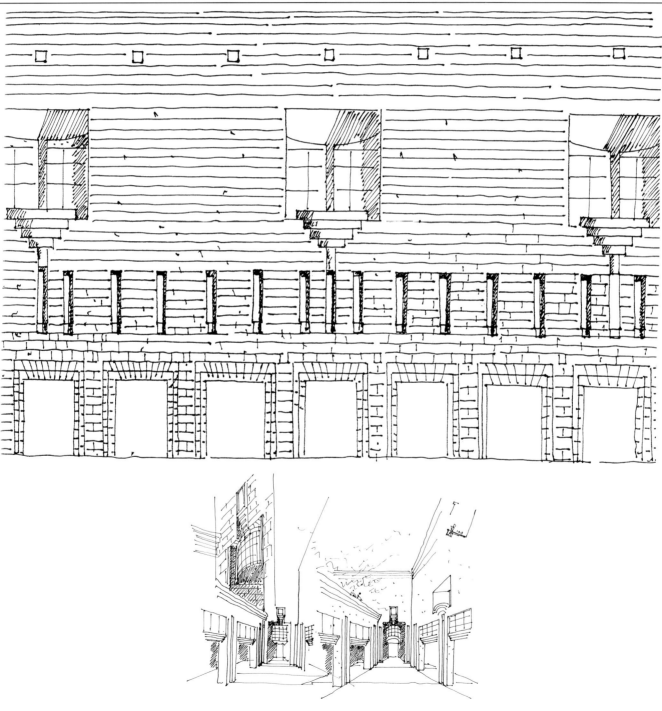

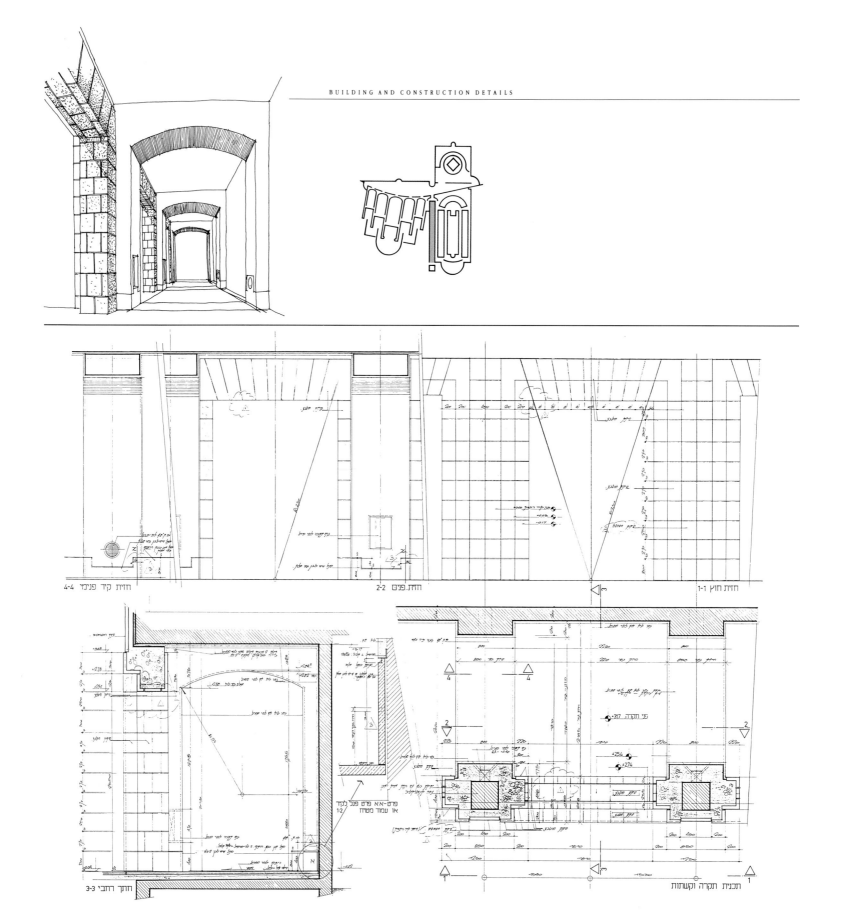

חתך רוחבי 3-3   פרט-או פרט פנל בלקד או עמוד מטויח 1-2   תכנית תקרה וקשתות 1

Plans and sections through arcades along the Knesset axis

Judges' Courtyard Elevation

The courtyard's longitudinal facade is double-layered. The outer skin is a 'traditional' stone construction; windows in the Administration wing peek out from the internal plastered skin. The sheltered and shady interstitial space acts as a passageway and a place for repose. The stone courtyard wall is a series of converging arches which create functional depths. The keystones, emphasized in the front, seemingly support the windows above.

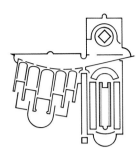

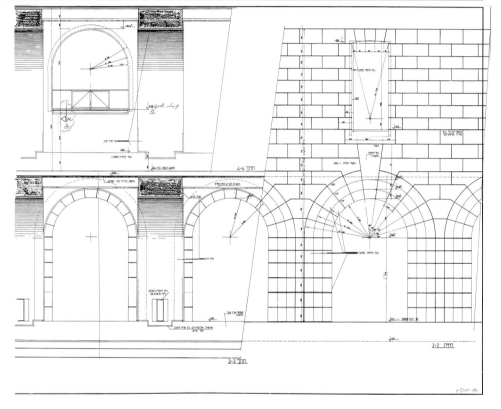

Arcades in the Judges' Courtyard

The inner plastered wall runs parallel to the
arched facade, creating deep recesses for sitting.
The level of the arcade is lower than that of the
Administration behind, creating the sensation of
a sunken room. The stone arches and the
plastered ones increase the volume and the
pace, as they elongate the perspective and
enrich the presence of the light within.

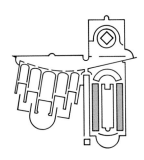

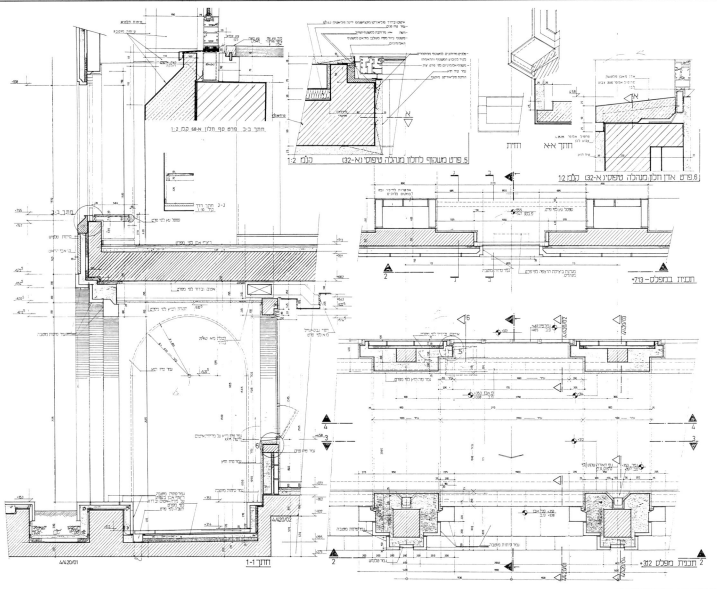

The Judges' Club

Suspended steel frames provide the structural skeleton for the plastered ceilings which are coated over an expanded metal lath.

The Judges' Courtyard: North Elevation

The plastered alcove is totally detached from the stone wall in plan and section. The separation creates a deep, utilitarian space, providing a secondary, private scale beyond the external stone arch.

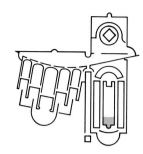

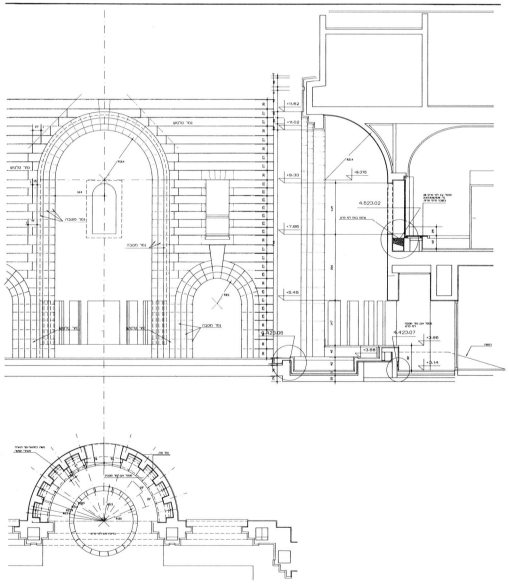

The Suspended Envelopes

The suspended elements have been utilized for the following purposes:

Suspended ceilings in the judges' chambers, club and large conference room

Volumetric elements comprising both ceiling and wall in the foyer and the library

A *'room within a room'* in the courtrooms, where the 'white' architecture is totally disengaged from the surrounding elements

The suspended plaster ceilings assume different forms throughout the building. They are a volumetric element which consists of a steel structure, an expanded metal lath and plaster coating, hanging from the concrete backing. The forms are usually emphasized by horizontal and vertical reveals where they join the wall. The reveals, often utilized for indirect lighting, accentuate the independence of ceilings and

walls. Plastering of the suspended ceilings was carried out in one stretch to avoid cracking.

1

2

3

5

6

4

1. Cross-vaulted ceiling in judge's chambers
2. G.R.C. arch
3. Indirect lighting
4. Completed plastered ceiling coated over expanded metal lath
5. Metal frame construction of barrel vaults in courtrooms
6. Mechanical system incorporated in ceiling

Judge's Chambers

The suspended vaults constitute an independent spatial element, detached from the concrete ceiling. Load transmission is expressed through the corners and cornices, as in traditional construction. The wall's volume is increased by 'load-bearing' gypsum partitions with deep niches, utilized for built-in furniture. Cross-vaulted ceilings are transformed into barrel-shaped vaults above the work area and the lounge area.

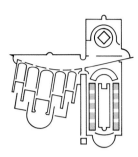

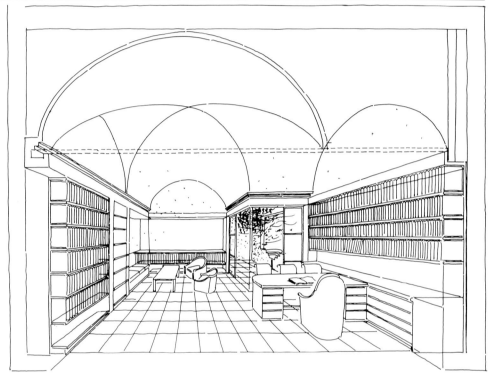

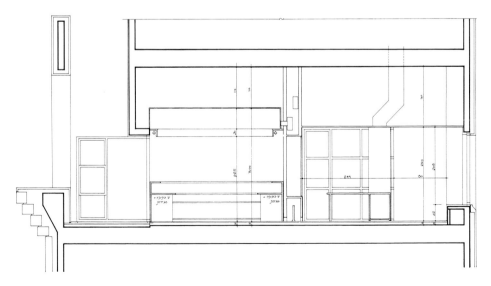

Section through judge's chamber and articled clerks' room

Judges' Level

1. Right: view of corridor leading to judges' chambers
2. Below left: section through secretarial offices and articled clerks' rooms
3. Judge's chambers corridor (alternative 2)
4. Detail of entrance to judge's chambers

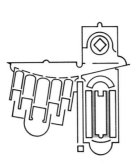

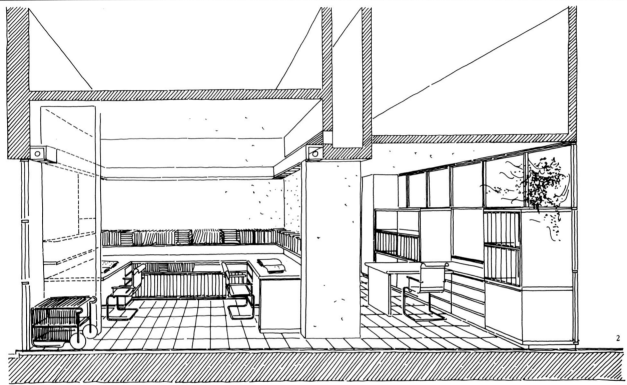

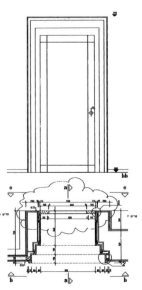

The Plastered Wall in the Grand Foyer

The foyer wall, like the library's 'drum' ceiling, is composed of two layers. From within the foyer the separation between the two is evident. The concrete backing ascends skyward; the plastered ceiling extends towards the courtrooms. An in-between space is formed, which tames the blinding light.

All along the foyer the contained space between the plastered ceiling and the concrete one is used as a technical 'floor.' Cylindrical metal elements inserted between the ceilings cause the light to ricochet within.

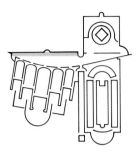

The Roof Level

The roof is the building's fifth elevation.
Its absolute height is identical to that of the
entrance to the Hilton Hotel. In the future, the
view from there will take in the archaeological
garden of modern architectural objects on the
Supreme Court roof. The garden of sculpted
forms and pure geometric figures is designed to
introduce light into the spaces beneath. This
technological elevation reads though its trans-
parencies, reflections and humour.

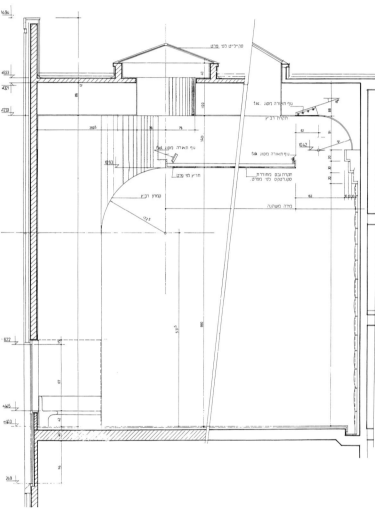

North-South section through grand foyer the stairway and panoramic window

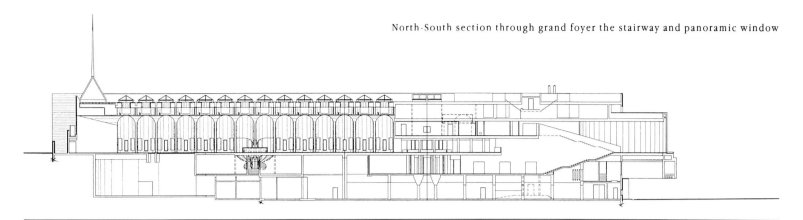

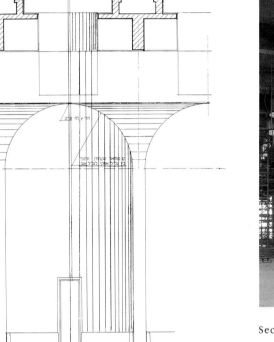

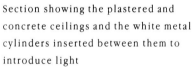

Section showing the plastered and concrete ceilings and the white metal cylinders inserted between them to introduce light

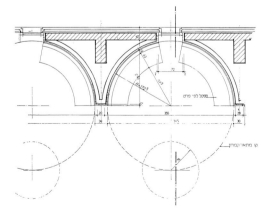

Plan at sitting level in Grand Foyer

155

The Library

The double layer 'drum wall' in the library space is composed of a vertical concrete backing and a plastered membrane. The skins recede from one another at library level. The inner skin forms a continuous, seamless wall which envelopes the entire library.

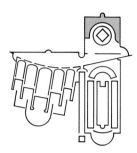

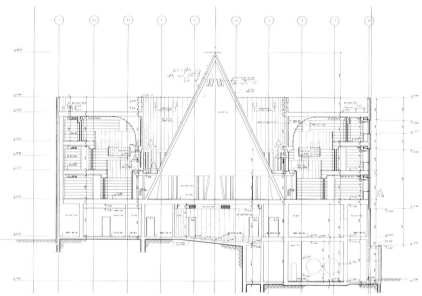

East-west section through pyramid and library

The Pyramid

The pyramid is a free-standing room inspired by light. It is surrounded by a multitude of layers (concrete, plaster, glass, wood and stone), blurring the boundaries between exterior and interior. The pyramid is both a space and an object. At the public level, it is experienced from within as an introverted white room. At the judges' level, seen from without, it is a free-standing, copper-clad object.

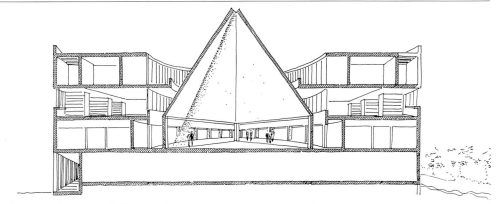

Early section through library, showing pyramid raised on columns

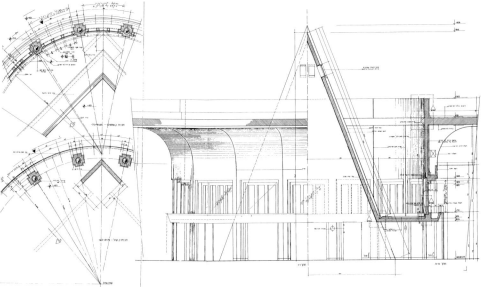

Section through pyramid, courtyard, external concrete wall and hung ceiling

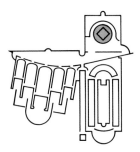

The Courtrooms

In the courtrooms, the plaster and stone walls are totally detached. Each courtroom is a white, introverted room protected by a stone room. The space between the two is utilized as a public passage and for absorbing and reflecting light. The enveloped space is symmetrical and static; the vertical enveloping space gravitates upwards.

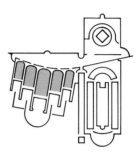

East-west section through courtrooms and Administration

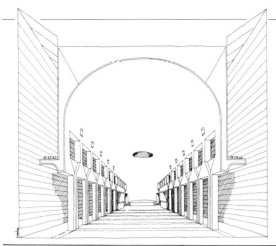

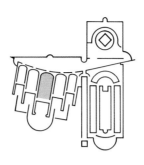

Large Courtroom (No. 3)

This is an independent, introverted, plastered room enveloped by an outer stone room. The space contained between these rooms is used for public circulation and indirect penetration of light. As in the other courtrooms, the centre of the stage is illuminated by direct natural light. The pattern of artificial light is designed to mimic that of the natural source: both emanate, directly or indirectly, from the same place.

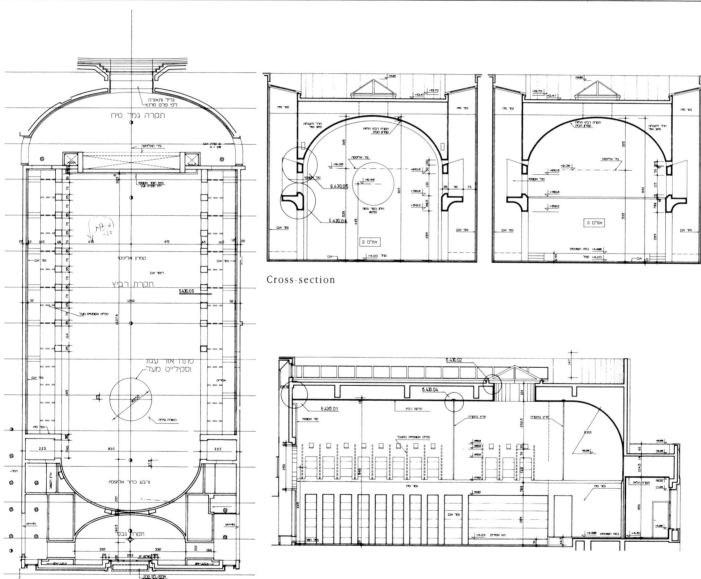

Plan at public level

Cross-section

Longitudinal section

161

The Small Courtroom (No. 1)

The courtroom is a continuous plastered surface supported by concrete walls. The natural light introduced through openings in the plaster membrane is soft and indirect.

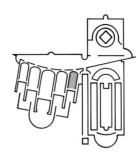

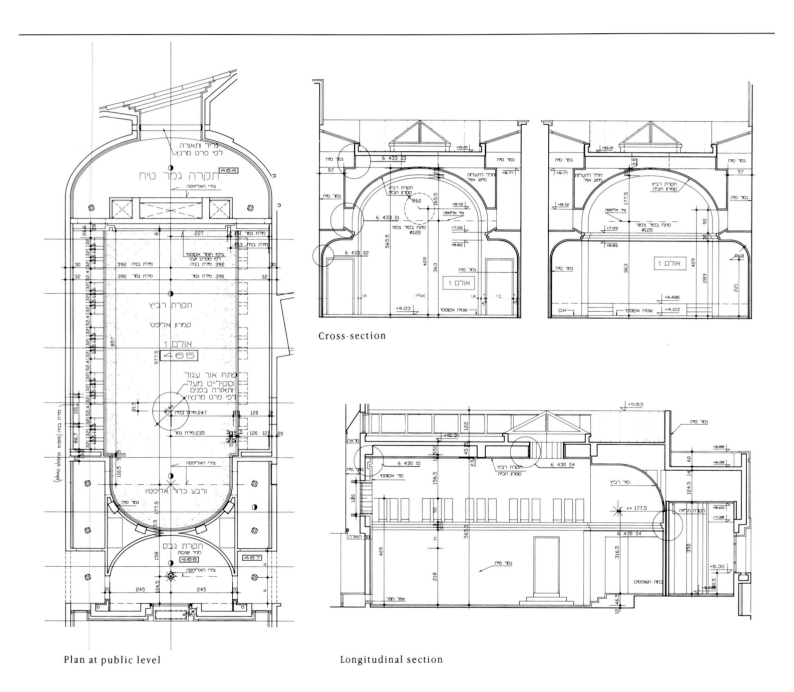

Plan at public level

Cross-section

Longitudinal section

162

Courtroom (No. 2)

The room is a free-standing object surrounded by stone walls. The cross-vaulted, suspended ceiling is framed by G.R.C. arches which transfer the load to the columns.

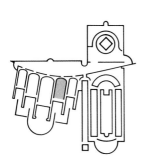

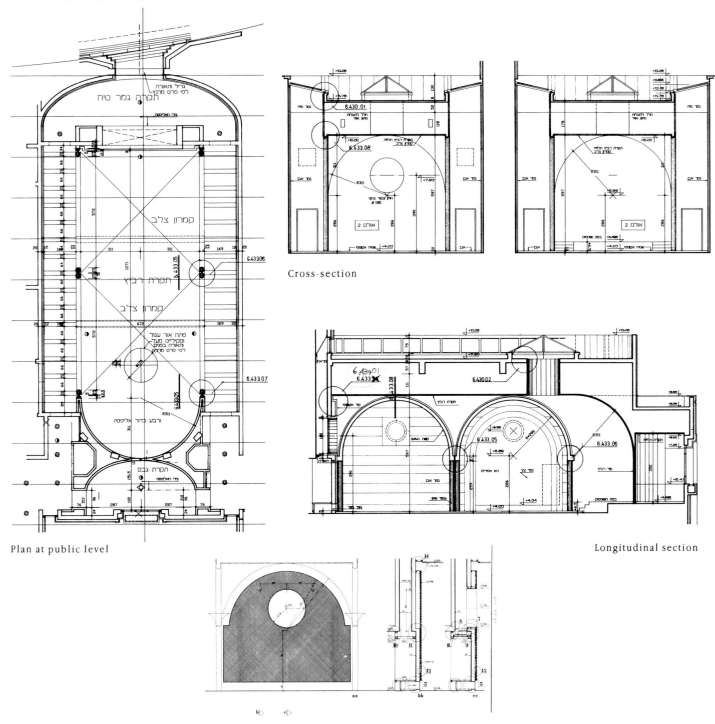

Plan at public level

Cross-section

Longitudinal section

Flooring Details

Throughout the building, the geometry of the floor tiles, the material and the hammering, vary. The overall geometry reflects the spatial sequence of the pattern of circulation. The nature of the material and chiseling are a function of the changing but continuous relationship between interior and exterior. The rougher flooring at the entrance is gradually refined, becoming more polished and articulated in the private sections of the building. Chiseled Mitzpe Ramon stone has been used at the entrance; in the pyramid there is a combination of hammered and polished stone. In the Grand Foyer, polished Atzmon stone is delineated by brass strips. At the judges' level, the flooring is composed of pink and grey marble from Vered Hagalil. The pyramid's floor, the most articulated of them all, consists of a palate of pastel-covered marble which gravitates towards the centre; divides of glass and brass describe the converging pyramid above. The design is by Tal Levy-Karmi.

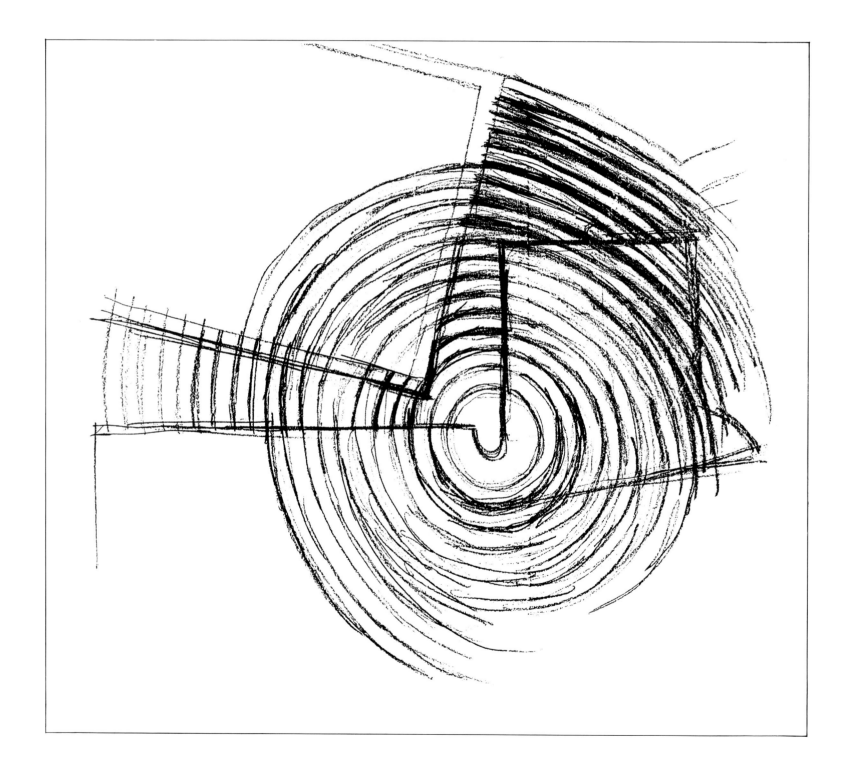

164

Coloured diagram of pyramid floor

Furniture Details

In each section of the building there is a distinct character to the materials employed. This is due mainly to the use of rough or hammered stone (for the building envelope and within) and to the junctions between the stone and the finer materials adjacent to it (plaster, gypsum, wood, etc.). The joints are generally accentuated by deep reveals, and occasionally by the introduction of foreign elements such as brass and glass, or painted aluminum.

The joints are similarly emphasized in both the interior design and in the furnishings. In addition to the delineation achieved through the use of brass, there is a pronounced seam between veneer and hard wood. The detailing of each piece of furniture responds to the standard available sizes of wood and veneer; reveals are utilized to articulate the personal and utilitarian scale.

In each section of the building there is something carried over from the preceding space. The building's variable component is the space itself and the means by which light is introduced. Together they bring out the palate of shades inherent in each material.

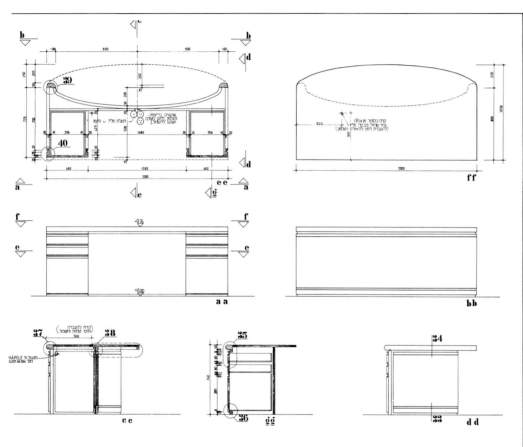

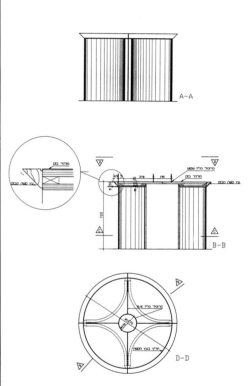

Desk in judge's chambers

Table in judge's conference area

Table in large conference room

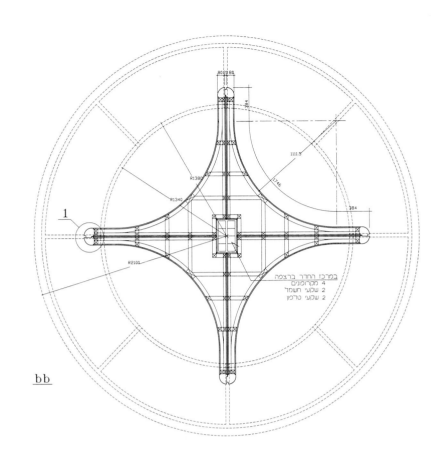

<u>bb</u>

במרכז החדר ברצפה
4 מקרופונים
2 שקעי חשמל
2 שקעי טלפון

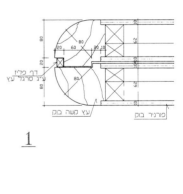

דף פליז
עץ סרגל עץ

עץ מושה בוק   פורניר בוק

<u>1</u>

<u>2</u>

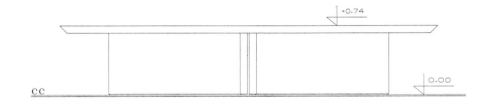

+0.74

<u>cc</u>

0.00

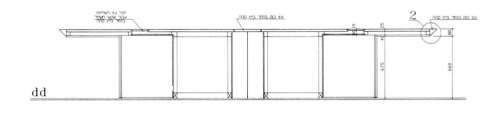

<u>dd</u>

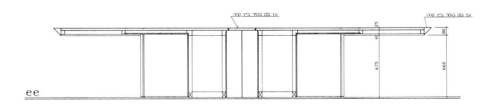

<u>ee</u>

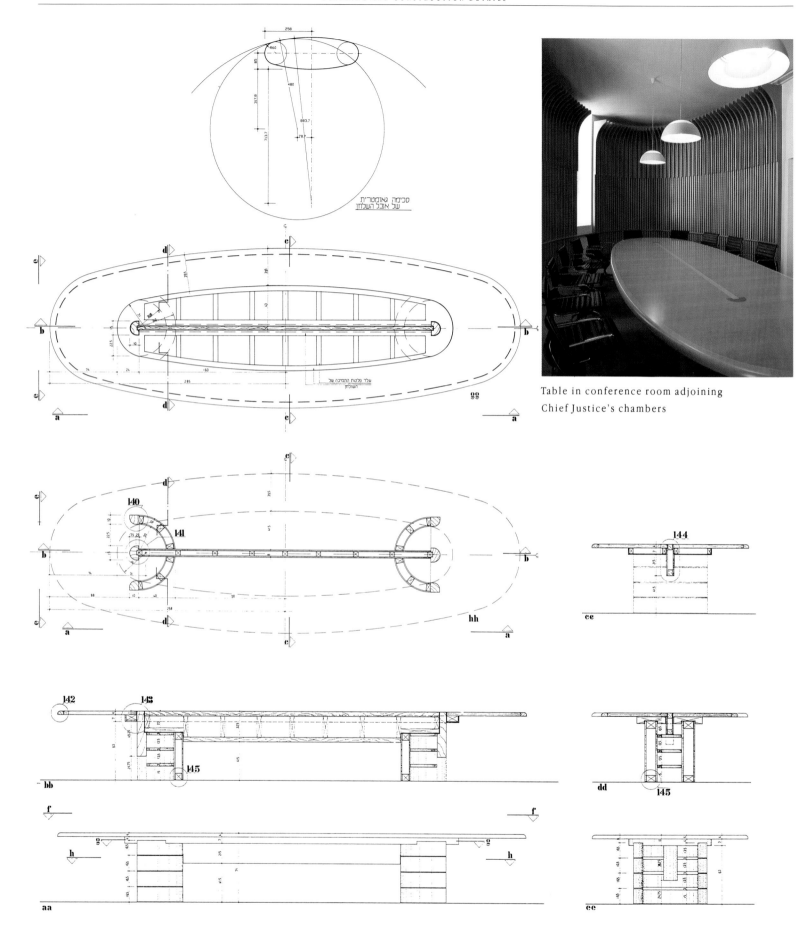

סכימה גאומטרית
של אובל השולחן

שלד מלכת התמיכה של
השולחן

Table in conference room adjoining
Chief Justice's chambers

Public benches in courtrooms

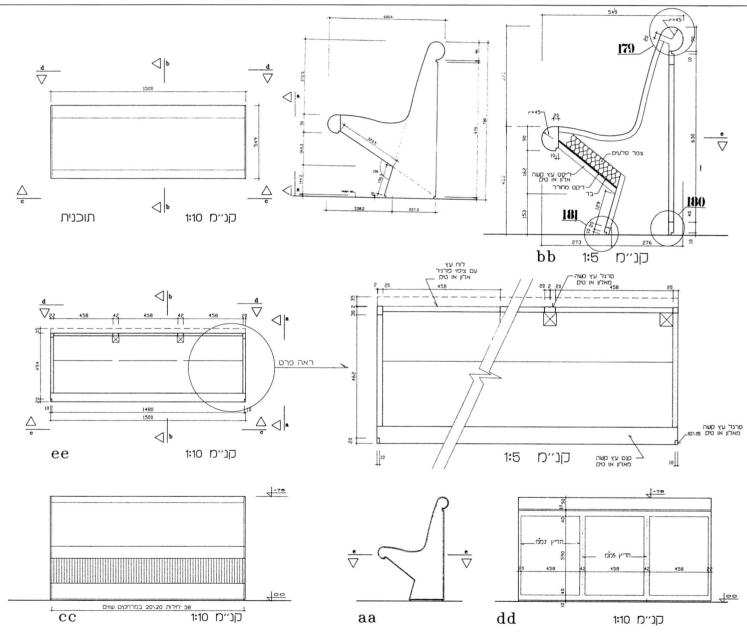

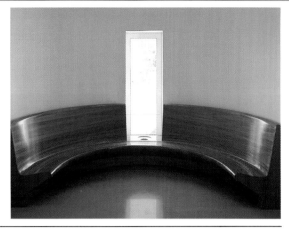

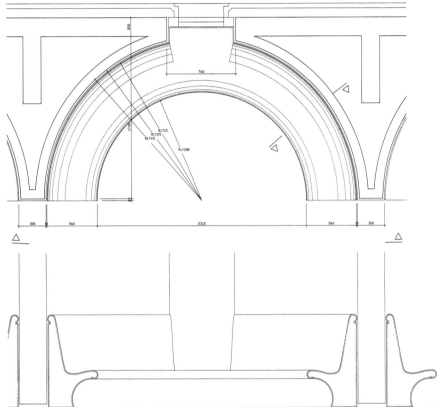

Public benches in Grand Foyer waiting area

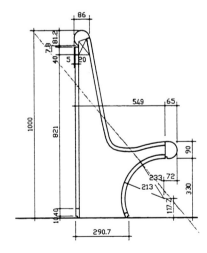

Lighting Details

Lighting along the main stairway is designed like a series of street lamps comprising pole, top-fitting and lamp housing. The pole is made of painted metal, terminating in engraved rings. The top-fitting is supported by an adjustable arched brass tube which includes a lighting element. The lighting element is made of oven-painted metal, with a reflecting element in the centre. The volumetric shape of the fixture is

derived from a geometric curve corresponding to the sides of the wall and the distance between fixture and wall.

In the courtrooms, the lighting fixtures conceal the seam between the supporting column and the arches. The fixture behaves as the column's capital and illuminates the cross-vaulted ceiling.

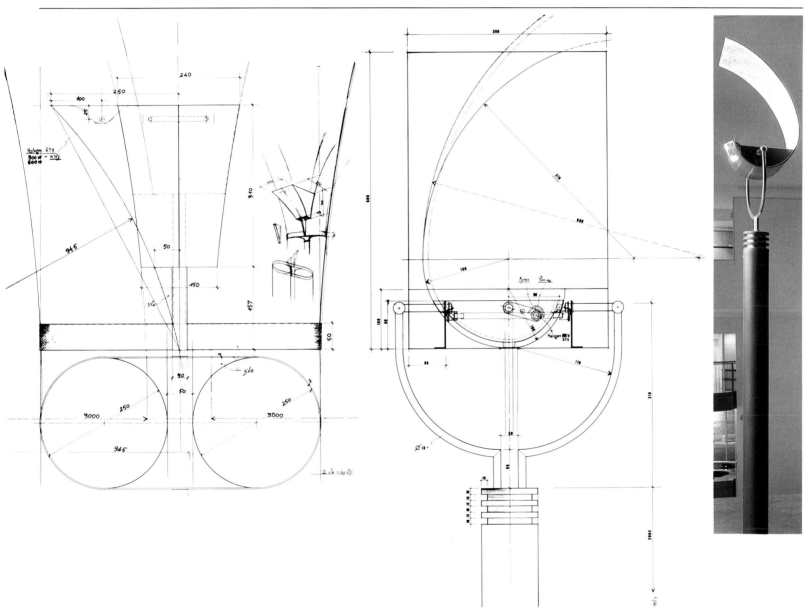

The Library's Internal Stairway

The library's metal stair is cantilevered from the
concrete floors and acts as a go-between for the
two upper tiers. Its continuous metal railing
encircles the perimeter of the library.

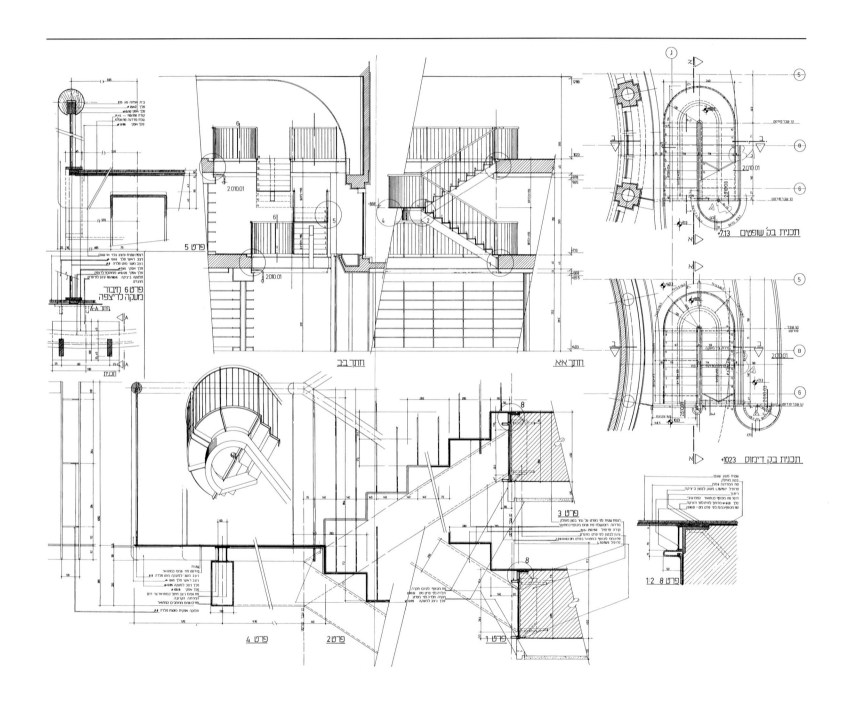

Details of Iron Railings in Library Stairway

1-2 Details of external main stairway

3 Details of internal library stairway

4 Section through curved perimeter edge showing
library stacks, lighting tube, metal-shielded
concrete floor and railing

5 Library stairway

1

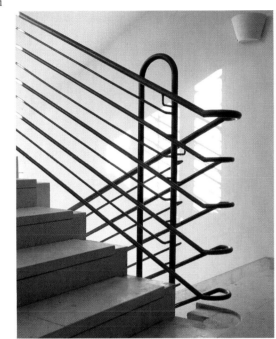

2

3

4

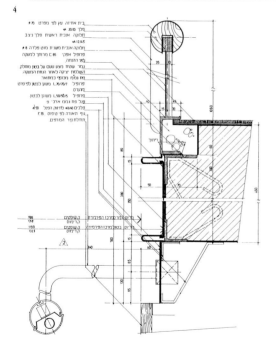

5

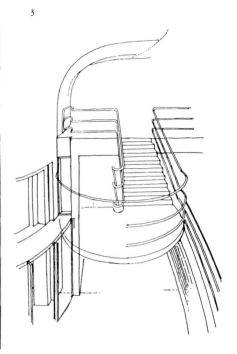

173

Graphics and Signage

Peter Szmuk and his associates' conception of the building's signs involves a modular projection of its characteristic elements. In designing a logo for the plaques, he used a square grid comprising nine smaller squares. The inspiration for the set number is derived from an engraving by the eighteenth century Dutch painter V. Vilalpandus, depicting the layout of the First Temple compound as a symmetrical structure divided into equal 'courts.'

A recurring motif appears throughout the sign system: square plaques for information and orientation, and rectangular ones for identification (names and positions). The square plaques include specially designed pictographs. The number of lines in each sign varies, although the top third is always in Hebrew (*Narkiss lettering*), the middle in Arabic (*Nadim*), and the lower third in English. In order to maintain a uniform appearance, *Fritzquadrant* was chosen for the Latin lettering (as its typography is closest to the Hebrew *Narkiss*), affording equal typographic weight to all three languages.

In the building's representative areas, the plaques are made of plexiglas and attached to the wall by plexiglas or aluminum cubes. The cubes represent architectural motifs or specific components of the building. Each form has been made by computer-controlled turning and sand blasting.

אבגדהוזחטיכךלמםנן
סעפףצץקרשת
1234567890".,

נרקיסים גודל 96 נקודות

ABCDEFGHIJKLMNOP
QRSTUVWXYZ
abcdefghijklmnopqrs
tuvwxyz
1234567890":.,

קוודרטה גודל 76 נקודות

مكاتب الحكام
مكتبة مكاتب

נאדים

174

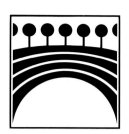

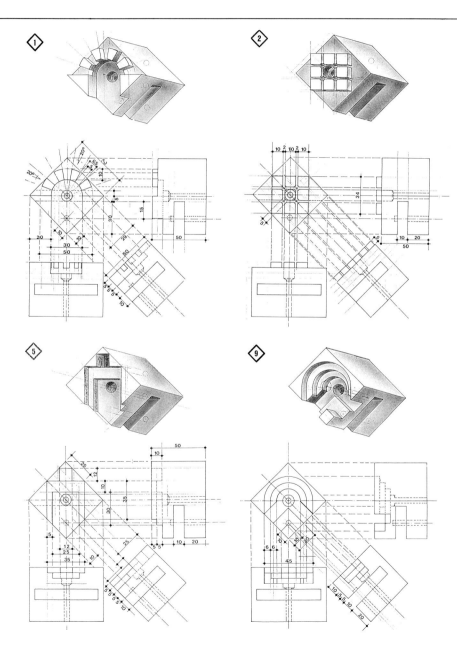

THE WHITE STONE

*T*he use of dressed and finely chiseled stone stresses the durability of public buildings of civic importance. As opposed to the hard granite and basalt rocks resulting from the rapid cooling of molten lava millions of years ago, the white limestone utilized in the Supreme Court Building is derived from precipitates of a prehistoric sea. Occasionally it contains fossils of marine plants, shells and even fish. Quarried in Mitzpe Ramon and later exposed to Jerusalem's dazzling light, after chiseling, the stone reflects a softer and more delicate, 'tamed' light.

At first, the planning team considered using a pink-colored stone (*Mizi Ahbar*) found at the site. When it was realized that no Israeli quarry could supply the necessary quantities, the possibility of importing it from Cyprus or Turkey was weighed. This may have been a realistic and inexpensive solution, but it was decided on principle to use local stone (*Mizi Yehudi*), the supply of which was assured. While more difficult to chisel than the pink rock, it weathers better. The planning team was confident that detail work would bring out its hues. They chose *Mesamsam* for the courtrooms and *Taltish Nakar* (rough) chiseling for the exterior walls. Arches and openings are chiseled in *Motabeh* (fine hammered) with minimal edging. The lower courses of the eastern and western walls of the library section are chiseled in *Tubzeh* which is even more rough than *Taltish Nakar*.

Due to the variety of chiseling styles and the fashioning of the arches to bring out the keystone benches and shaded apses, the stone assumed a rich texture. As the light changes during the day, so does the appearance of the stone: the light accents its dressing and lends the monotone white a dramatic appearance.

AFTERWORD

*T*he architects' status was analogous to that of a lawmaker. They proposed a coherent architectural statement, which they refined and developed. The architects' ongoing dialogue with Yad Hanadiv and the Supreme Court nurtured it to maturity. The building testifies that sound architectural concepts need not be rigid and constricted. In fact, strong and meaningful conceptions are more readily refined and developed. In the case of the Supreme Court, the results are faithful to the architects' design.

In the design development stage, the architects selected materials that would generate a distinct contrast between massive archaic elements and modern ones (e.g. the molded white backbone). This juxtaposition constitutes a major contribution to Israeli architecture.

The architects' consideration of the various alternatives came to an end once they adopted and reinterpreted the urban principle of the Cardo and the Decumanus. This led to the introduction of the massive stone wall which divides the building into north and south. Later, the public access from the garden to the south (where the cafeteria and the amphitheater are now located) was eliminated. Unlike in the original draft, the public enters the courtrooms via the grand foyer, immediately after passing through the pyramid. In the building's present form, the foyer is the 'main attraction.' According to Ram Karmi.

> "The building's last and most important station – the courtrooms – is quieter than
> the foyer itself, which has seemingly stolen the show. If the public had had to pass
> through the garden, the encounter with the Supreme Court would have been a more
> dramatic one. The tension would have subsided in the garden, but upon entering
> the courtrooms, it would have gradually built up again. Today, on the other hand,
> the Supreme Court is a 'buttoned-down' public building and I like it even though
> this meant foregoing an element which provided some respite from the formalistic
> language."

Another, and no less dramatic, confrontation was included in each of the alternatives: the pattern of circulation within the building whisks the public up from the entrance to the panoramic window. Here the view of the City is not an afterthought on the way to the judicial process, but rather one of the important links of the architectural discourse taking place. The forceful presence of Jerusalem seemingly emphasizes the reciprocal relations between the law and all that lies beyond it. According to the architects' perception, the law is not a mechanical application of an abstract principle. Nor is the application of the principles of justice in the courtrooms carried out in an historical and cultural 'void.' Whoever enters the building to seek law and justice cannot overlook the Supreme Court's complex affinity to tradition, the architectural emphases, or the multiple links to Jerusalem. Wherever one turns, one carries along this 'view of the City.'

Throughout the building, the architects availed themselves of analogies couched in materials and forms commensurate with their perception of law and order. The respect accorded judicial authority is also expressed in the attempt to relate to verbal sources of inspiration; more than once (particularly in preparing the competition entry), the written word preceded architectural solutions and choices of 'style.' However, architectural forms cannot preserve the nuances of verbal images. Every architect who 'recapitulates' the past is well aware that he cannot use architectural 'statements' to convey verbal messages.

Ada Karmi-Melamede and Ram Karmi considered that several of the Biblical metaphors relating to law and justice are fraught with inspiration for architectural concepts. Even though justice is 'invisible' to the human eye, the circle described in Psalms gave the architects the opportunity, in various parts of the Supreme Court Building, to allude to an affinity between the biblical source and the 'pure' architectural form.

The architectural elements and their wide symbolic aspects echo our high expectations to live in an enlightened and just society. It would be prudent to point out that civic buildings, important as they may be, are not intended to be 'worshipped,' but to be used and to convey a concept greater than their physical boundaries. A fine line must be drawn: I hope that I have been cautious in interpreting the architects' intentions and have not rendered the building as an awesome monument. My sole wish was to promote this architectural creation.

Yossi Sharon

SOME OF THE PERSONALITIES INVOLVED IN THE PROJECT

CONSULTANTS, SUPPLIERS AND CONTRACTORS

Client: Yad Hanadiv

Architects: Karmi Architects, Ltd. – Ada Karmi-Melamede and Ram Karmi
Project Coordinator: Meir Drezner
Design Team: Iftach Issacahrov, Simon Friedman, Alan Aranoff, Ruth Rotholtz-Van Eck, Daniel Azerrad, Motty Shyovitz, Rami Yogev, Tzadik Eliakim, Zvi Dunsky, Dan Price and Tal Gazit

Construction Management and Coordination: E. Rahat Engineering
Management Coordination Jerusalem
Director: Eliezer Rahat
Team for Coordination, Administration, Supervision of Building and Electromechanical Systems: Moti Kobi, Yigael Kurtzweil, Anne Mintz-Cohen, Dimitry Perlin, Shimon Yerushalmi

Yad Hanadiv Architectural Consultant: Arthur Spector

Early Planning, Permitting and Budget Consultants: Dan Wind and Partners, Ltd.
Principal: Dan Wind
Project Coordinator: Gil Gordon

Land Consultant: David David

Geologist: Uzi Zaltzman

General Contractor: G.G. Peretz Engineers, Jerusalem
Principals: Gabriel Peretz, Giora Peretz
Staff: Yosef Hershtik, Nimrod Madmoni, Bassam Rimoury, Moshe Brodetsky, Zion Regev

Land Development – Parking, Rose Garden Road, Access Road: M. Barashi and Sons

Structural Engineers: Dr. Eliyahu Traum, Haifa

Air Conditioning Consultant: B. Schorr & Co. Consulting Engineers

Electrical System Consultant: G. Itkin – E. Blum Electrical Engineers

Lighting Consultant: Jules Fisher and Paul Marantz, Inc., New York

Plumbing Consultant: A. Yosha Consulting Engineers, Jerusalem

Acoustics Consultant: Shimon Greenbaum, Herzlia

Graphics and Signage Design: Peter Szmuk, Tel Aviv

Insulation/Sealants Consultant: M. Marton

Roofs on Wings 1, 2, 3: A. Halperin Ltd.

Waterproofing of Flower Beds: D.C.S. Systems

Waterproofing of Outer Walls: Sheratol

Insulation of Inducts Against Fire: Techno-Handassah Ltd.

Insulation of Roofs of Courtrooms: Haogenplast

Aluminum Consultant: Y. Landman

Kitchen Design: Nachshon – Food Facilities Consultants

Initial Programme Consultant: Enosh, Ramat Gan

General Surveying: Dotan – Cooperman Surveyors, Ramat Gan

Building Surveying: M. Heller, Shiba, Zichron Ya'acov

Safety: A. Arnan, Beer Sheva

Communications: I. Leshem, Shachak Communications, Kiryat Ono

Maintenance: R. Waltman

Access Road: S. Buengo

Roads: M.T.N., A. Sumir

Infrastructure: Excavation Works: Ha'levyim Ltd.; On-site Office: Barton; Fences: Iskoor; Erection of Fences: Lev Habayit; Microplies: Ha'mephatel (1993); G.R.C.: G.R.C. Products; Precast Units for Parking: Clal Cement Ltd.; Copper Roof of Pyramid: A. Uziel; Reinforcing Contractor: Shimon Abutbul; Plaster Contractor: Mordecai Cohen

Stone and Stone Masonry: Jerusalem Marble, Y. Grabelsky and Yiftach Marble; Stone Stairs: Peles; Stone Floors: M. Benjo Ltd.; Rough Stone and Dry Mounting of Stone in Courtrooms: Hazitot; Mosaic Mounting and Stone Work: Eitan Frenkel Ltd.; Flooring: Sdot Yam Tiles, Kibutz Sdot Yam; Flooring in Cafeteria and Washrooms and Tiling in Kitchen: Maiman Services Ltd.

Metal Works: Copper and Brass Work: D. Stein and AMIK; Steel Works and Structure for Special Plaster: Y. Goren; Metal Industries and Uruguay Metal Works

Hardware Consultant and Supply: Interbuild Ltd.

Landscape Consultant: H. Kahanovitch

Landscaping: Dan Arman Ltd.

Rose Garden Landscaping: Green Gan

Fire Detection System: Afkon Control and Automation Ltd.

Paintwork: Special Paint Reinforced by Fiberglass: ISA-Israel Scandinavian Agency Ltd.; Special Paint: Nadir and Kristal Paint Works (1981) Ltd.; General Paint: Hativ Paint Works Ltd.

Gypsum Board: Rappaport Technologies

Aluminum and Glass Work: Aluminum and Glass: Alumeir Ltd.; Bulletproof Glass: Oran, Kibbutz Tzuba; General: F. Kramer Ltd.

Electromechanical Works: Electrical Works: A. Feuchtwanger Ltd.; Sanitation Works: Herut Ltd.; Air Conditioning Works: Own Ltd.

Lighting Fixtures: Steinitz Lighting Industries Ltd.; Lev Ophir Group; Kimchi Lighting Ltd.; L. Poulsen – Denmark; Zumtobel – Austria

Doors: Talpiot Wood

Furniture: Entrance Desk, Courtrooms, Various Tables: Galil Furniture; Attorneys' Rooms: S. Ephraim; Administration: B. Keidar; Judges' Chambers and Library: A.D. Segal Industries 1986 Ltd.; Benches in Courtrooms and Various Tables: Braun Carpentry Ltd.; Bookstands and Cupboards: Wilstein Ltd.; Administration: Finish – Schwartz Bros.; Chairs in Administration, Registry and for Articled Clerks: Tzora Furniture; Chairs in Auditorium: Waxman Bros.; Control-Room Counter: Efrat Ltd.; Library Chairs: Modulus Ltd., Fritz Hansen – Denmark; Chairs for Judges, Judge's Meeting Rooms and Library: Poltrona Frau, Cassina and Alivar – Italy, Herman Miller, Knoll – England (Importers: Tollman's, Habitat Office Furniture, Modulus Ltd. – Israel, Aram Design – England, GF Office Furniture – U.S.A.) Book Trucks for Library: Gaylord Bros.; Tables in Judges' Meeting Room: Tollman's and Frank Lloyd Wright

Carpets: Golde Carpets; Carmel Carpets; Shoham Decoration; Decorative Rugs: Eli Sasson, Tel Aviv and Moshe Kattan, Jerusalem

Security Systems: Closed Circuit Television System: Elbex Video Ltd.; Magnometer in Library: Check Point Systems Ltd.; Gate System: Gousinsky Engineering and Manufacturing Co. Ltd.; Peripheral Security System: Afkon Control Automation Ltd.; Communication Systems: Telrad Telecommunications and Electronics Industries Ltd.; Intercom and Loudspeaker System: Ramtel Communication Systems Ltd.

Kitchen: Termokor Cooling and Engineering (1978); Kitchen Equipment: Nirocenter Ltd.

Preparation of Tenders: I.P.M. Ltd.

Copies of Plans: Or; Sephigraph; Aminograph; Li Gal Graph

Site Security: Mor Engineering Maintenance and Safety Jerusalem Ltd.

Genie Lift and Metal Scaffolding: Amir Ltd.

Signs: Cna'an Productions Ltd.

Accessories: Halom shel Halon; Kub Kol; Lo-ly

Draperies: Nussbaum Ltd.

Upholstery: Tempelhoff Upholstery

Hanging of Paintings and Draperies: M. Cabasso

Glass in Pyramid Floor: Langford Glass Ltd.

Ritual Handwashing Sink in Cafeteria: Mandil Bros. Marble

Parking Markings: Merkom Ltd.

Ceramic Tiles: Shemer

APPENDIX

Statement of Intent Submitted by the Architects to the Architectural Competition

Law courts were historically situated at the 'city gates.' This strategic location had a symbolic importance essential to an orderly and democratic society. The law calibrates the relationship between the individual and the collective through mutual agreement. This bond results from a common history and tradition and seems to respond to a profound need for order.

We viewed the Supreme Court Building symbolically as an equation between two forces: the law restricting the individual within society and the law protecting individual rights.

In this spirit we chose to surround the building with a simple stone wall so that it becomes an integral part of the natural landscape. The use of stone expresses the 'genius loci' rather than a purely functional criterion. The Supreme Court Building should project a dignified image which conveys the notion that justice must be seen to be done. These ideas ought to be articulated in built form in order to become part of the collective memory. Analogous to the legal process which relies on precedents and discretionary judgments – architecture draws on existing Jerusalem archetypes and tries to imbue them with new meaning.

The Supreme Court Building should derive its personality from its place in the historical and cultural context and its location in the urban fabric, its topography and site.

Historical Context

The importance of 'the book' in the history of the Jewish people created a tradition of justice, humanism and abstract thought. The spiritual dimension of the Supreme Court Building is reflected through the primacy of the library in the building's organization. In contrast, the courtrooms should visually reflect the tangible involvement of the people with their land and the perception that tradition and landscape are inseparable. Architecture in Jerusalem has always been challenged by its historical context. Architects aspired to find a

language appropriate to its time and place and strove to develop a typology which would mediate between historical tradition and contemporary ideas. They resorted to an almost classical statement which withstood the test of time.

Urban and Topographical Context

Government hill (the National Precinct) is the stage of a natural amphitheater in western Jerusalem, of which the Supreme Court Building occupies the geographic centre. At present this is a barren 'no-man's-land.' It is surrounded by government buildings isolated from one another by security zones and parking areas. The single element linking these domains is an asphalt loop road which, paradoxically, is the only symbol of their functional unity. During working hours this complex is occupied, only to become deserted at night and on holidays. We, therefore, felt that the Supreme Court Building should become the keystone between the City and the government complex.

The building is situated at the intersection of various axes:

• The green east/west belt which connects Sacher Park, the Wohl Rose Garden and the Givat Ram Campus of the Hebrew University – an informal axis which will generate public activity outside of working hours;

• The north/south axis running along the ridge which connects the Central Bus Station (city gate), Binyaney Ha'ooma (The Jerusalem Convention Centre), the Hilton Hotel, the Knesset and the Israel Museum.

• The axis extending between the Old City and Government Hill establishes a dialogue between the spiritual and secular centres of Israel. The urban manifestation of this axis is already evident. It extends between the Rockefeller Museum and the Rose Garden, stringing together many of the important public places in the city: Damascus Gate, the Russian Compound, Zion Square, Ben Yehuda

Mall and the Supreme Court site. This axis extends further to the west – to Mt. Scopus, and further to the east – to the National Library and Mt. Herzl. Once this axis is formally articulated it will strengthen the ties between the two parts of the city.

Therefore, this building cannot be viewed merely as a single freestanding object in the landscape, but should relate both to its immediate environment and to the larger urban context. Our intention is to create a harmonious relationship between the executive, legislative and judicial institutions and also to create a public place which is part of a larger sequence.

Movement Patterns in the Building

Public movement towards the building and within is a combination of circular and linear patterns. The intent is to give a clear geometric expression to values of justice and law. Justice is described in the Bible as a circle while law is described as a line.

A grand circular movement which generates from the entry is reinforced by the configuration of the curved library above. This movement is dramatically transformed by the disposition of the courtrooms into a single linear axis.

Functionally, the building is divided into two systems: horizontal and vertical. The former provides the link between the different domains within the building and defines the boundary between interior and exterior. The latter creates the hierarchy of public and private domains and sets up the visual tension between them.

The Gate and the Entrance Hall

Jerusalem is a city of gates and walls. In our building plan the gate is a free-standing element set in a protected forecourt. People arriving by public or private transportation are gathered along a covered pedestrian path which 'equalizes' everyone before the law. The approach towards the gate is direct and frontal. The gate is an extended threshold allowing a gradual transition between inside and out. The legal administration is located at the entry in order to differentiate between the building's ceremonial and administrative functions. All bureaucratic procedures are carried out at entry level. (806)

From here, up a familiar Jerusalem stone alley, one ascends towards a window, where a panoramic view of the city is revealed. The window acts as a turning point from which one confronts the actual entrance hall. This space is reminiscent of Absalom's Tomb, it is testimony to the durability of law through time. The pure geometrical form of this room tapers towards the apex, allowing light to penetrate its volume. It is a static and serene space which detaches the sacred from the profane. This is the true 'gatehouse' of the Supreme Court Building. The height of this space links the public level (809) with the library (812) and the Chief Justice's Section (815). The library, defined by a curved facade, embraces the 'gatehouse.' It is perceived as the very memory of the judicial tradition. Here, centuries of legal tradition, encompassing the principles of social justice and moral values, are preserved to ensure protection of the weak from the strong. The prominent position of the library and its specific relationship to the 'gatehouse' express its independence and its role as guardian. The Judges' Section is linked to the library by a bridge which crosses over the 'Jerusalem stone alley' through which one enters the building. The library, organized in small intimate alcoves lined with books, overlooks the 'gatehouse.' This relationship accentuates the unique role of the library in this building.

Level 809 fulfills the building's, non-programatic elements. It caters solely to the public, with a view to enriching their experience in a dignified and respectful way. It generously offers places of different moods – places of learning, of waiting, of strolling, of repose and expectation. We felt that the Judges' Courtyard might also be used in the future by the public and, therefore, introduced a potential exhibit area along its perimeter.

The Judges' Chambers and Courtyard

The Judges' Courtyard is formed by two parallel rows of chambers surrounded by a stone wall. An axial opening offers a visual connection with the outside landscape and the Knesset. Each chamber is elevated from the courtyard level and assumes its own spatial presence. The chambers open individually onto the courtyard through a private patio

and a small window. This type of layering allows for seclusion and introspection. The glare is diffused by the greenery of the individual patios. The courtyard is made exclusively of stone, broken only by a narrow channel of water on the central axis. The stone quarried from the earth, and the water reflecting the sky, juxtapose Biblical symbols of truth and justice. The spirit of the Judean Desert and of Jerusalem is hewn into the stone; it is harsh and uncompromising in its stark beauty – a courtyard of motionless silence.

The Courtrooms and the Walled Garden

The courtrooms are separated from the Judges' Section. The intent was to create a significant distance between the place of public hearing and judgment, and the place of contemplation and deliberation. The courtrooms are raised above ground (812) creating intimate waiting areas underneath, which lead off to the walled garden – a place for repose. The judges enter the courtrooms directly from 812. The public ascends to the courtrooms from 809 while the prisoners descend from 815.

The courtrooms appear set in niches formed by the natural terrain. They are faced with smooth marble, in contrast to the rough stone of the retaining walls. Both the physical space between these walls and the use of different materials express the independence of the courtrooms nestling in the hill.

In contrast to the brilliant light of the Judges' Courtyard, the reflected light in the courtroom area is soft and tranquil. Indirect light washes down between the retaining walls and the courtrooms, suggesting green and shade – the mood of paradise lost.

Conclusion

The Supreme Court Building ought to be a cultural and visual symbol. Yet it is an introverted walled-in building, characteristic of Jerusalem architecture. Its particular ritual is revealed layer by layer through an architecture of procession. It forms an integral part of the landscape, presenting a powerful and serene architectural image, unique to Jerusalem.